The Naked
Christian

The Naked
Christian

Taking off religion
to find true
relationship

Craig
Borlase

[RELEVANTBOOKS]

Published by Relevant Books
A division of Relevant Media Group, Inc.

www.relevantbooks.com
www.relevantmediagroup.com

Design by Relevant Solutions
Cover design by Ben Pieratt, Jeremy Kennedy
Interior design by Aaron Maurer, Jeremy Kennedy

Library of Congress Control Number: 2005902177
International Standard Book Number: 0-9760357-7-4

For information or bulk orders:
RELEVANT MEDIA GROUP, INC.
100 SOUTH LAKE DESTINY DR. STE. 200
ORLANDO, FL 32810
407-660-1411

05 06 07 08 9 8 7 6 5 4 3 2 1

Printed in the United States of America

TO EMMA: WITH WHOM NUDITY IS FAR LESS SCARY

Contents

Foreword

by Mike Pilavachi

This is an unusual book. It is not written by someone in the forefront of Christian ministry. In fact, Craig is a full-fledged schoolteacher. So what qualifies Craig to write a book that others will find worth reading?

Actually, you may vaguely recognize his name. He has helped a number of speakers, including myself, put our thoughts into writing. While the likes of Andy Hawthorne, Matt Bird, David Westlake, and myself have seen our names with the larger lettering on the front covers, I know that at least in my case Craig has been so much more than a ghostwriter. In fact, more than once have I found myself a fictional character in my own books, a figment of Craig's mercurial imagination!

I first met Craig when he was thirteen years old, and I became his youth pastor. He writes in *The Naked Christian* honestly and compellingly of the battles with the faith of his youth. He writes of his struggles with the institution of the Church and of her seeming inability to communicate relevantly to either himself or his friends. Craig "went walkabout" from his faith and from the Church for a few years and got involved in a world which was very different from the one he grew up in. He then describes his journey back, although he would be the first to correct me for using that expression. In a very real sense it has not so much been a journey back as a "journey through." He has certainly not returned to the faith of his childhood but has come to a quite different faith, one that is real, thought-through, and, while still childlike, no longer childish.

Why is it important to read Craig's story? Because it is well written, thoughtful, reflective, and often humorous. Because it has insight into some of the nonsense and empty religiosity practiced in the Church. More than any of the above, it is important because Craig is articulating many of the questions, the frustrations, and the pain of a generation that has been lost to the Church. It also gives us an understanding as to why many in Craig's generation will not even dream of looking to the Church for answers to their questions or healing for their lives.

Finally, Craig has talked openly of his pain, which he not only found no healing for in the Church but which was also at times dealt to him by the Church. It grieves me to say that I was one of those who caused his greatest pain. As his youth leader I responded incredibly badly to his questions, judged him for his lifestyle, and refused to see what lay behind his behavior. I know I wounded him terribly. It is the pure grace of God and Craig's capacity for forgiveness that he is now one of my closest friends, he and his wife, Emma, valued members of the congregation I pastor, and an indispensable colleague in the ministry.

I now have my brother back. It is my prayer that this honest, beautifully written, and, in the best sense of the word, uncomfortable book will help us to understand so that we do not carelessly and unthinkingly lose another generation.

—Mike Pilavachi

"Obedience, sacrifice, and relationship—the real twinkles in God's eye."

1

What Do I Want to Look Like?

The Myth of the Spiritual Six-Pack

So here I am, the Naked Christian. Standing in front of the mirror, baring all, clothes scattered on the floor around me. This is what my faith really looks like. This is what I believe, what I worry about, what I hope for. This is the real me: undressed from all the attitudes and beliefs that I wear in public. There's no hiding, no pretense. OK, so I may be sucking the flabby stomach in a bit, but this is about as close to the real me as I can get. It feels odd at first, seeing everything so exposed, but good, too. I'm reminded of how it felt when I started learning to drive, when just sitting in the driving seat felt so magnetic, so euphoric, so full of potential. Where will this journey of discovery take me?

But as I stand and stare, taking the reflection in, looking over the contours of my stripped-down faith, a deeper, heavier feeling takes over. Gradually being naked doesn't feel so exciting. I look at myself, and what do I see? An imperfect body. I've got a clear image of how I'd like to look, but the Christian in the mirror in front of me is a long way off.

Ah yes, you say. We all fall short of perfection. Isn't that a part of every Christian, the idea of being aware of the sickness of our sin and the health of God's holiness? True enough, but somehow I know there's a slightly different image of perfection that's drifting around in my mind. Sure, I want that sin-free health, but I feel the pressure to want something altogether different as well. I feel the need for a six-pack. A rippling, rock-hard wall of stomach muscle, a show-it-off-in-public six-pack. Holiness may be healthy, but I want to look sexy.

Let me explain. For years I wondered what on earth God was going to do with my life, what I was going to achieve, what was going to mark me out as special for Him. Then I heard The Talk. Given by a healthy, wealthy, and deeply tanned Californian, I learned how it was not only OK but essential to "dream dreams for God." Kick back on the sofa, we were told, and let your mind wander to a better place. Picture yourself doing something truly great for God, something amazing, something remarkable. Tell God that's what you want and "pray it into reality." Over the years I've spent days on end praying and dreaming about what I'd like to do for God. I've wanted to be a preacher, pacing the stage and whipping the gathered masses with devastatingly profound revelations about God. I've wanted to be a worship leader, making jaw-droppingly cool music that sends everyone wild. I've wanted to be a writer, steaming straight to the top of the bestseller list with my inspiring brand of biting satire. All great things. All sexy things. All marks of the spiritual six-pack.

But then I heard something that made me think. I was talking to a friend, who told me something profound. We were chatting about that bit in the Bible where Jesus talks about two teams of people, the sheep and the goats, with the sheep getting the thumbs-up from the King and the goats getting the wave goodbye. What made the difference between the two—apart, I presume, from the fact that the sheep would make better knitwear—was the way they responded to the hungry, the thirsty, the strangers, the poor, the sick, and the prisoners. The ones who failed to feed, clothe, and visit were told:

"I tell you the truth, whatever you did not do for one of the least of these, you did not do for me. Then they will go away to eternal punishment, but the righteous to eternal life" (Matt. 25:45-46).

"The way I see it," said my friend, "you can't call yourself a Christian if you're ignoring the poor, the sick, and the oppressed. And that scares me."

It scared me, too. What did this mean? Were my dreams of doing great things for God not enough? Was there a chance that I might end up on the goat team, despite the fact that I was the funniest, funkiest, and most spiritual goat around? Looking back I still haven't worked out exactly how I feel about this "ignoring the poor = straight to hell" line of thought, especially when the question of grace and forgiveness is thrown into the mix, but that's not the point. The truth is that it made me think: My ambitions were out of sync. I'd come so far down the line of believing in the importance of doing great things for God that my idea of spiritual success had become about as deep and meaningful as a real life gym-bunny body. I mean, looking like Brad or Jennifer might be nice, but it would hardly make any of us better people. And so it was with my spiritual workout; I was aiming for the wrong thing altogether. Instead of viewing godly success as obedience, sacrifice, and relationship with our Maker, I'd been convinced that it was found in influence, fame, and recognition.

The Spiritual Six-Pack

We see it everywhere we look. OK, so we might not have the highly developed media network in the Christian scene that exists in mainstream culture, but the pressure to conform to industry standards is there just as strong. Instead of spreads in British publications *OK!* and *Hello* where the stars show us around "their own" homes, displaying their perfect lifestyles, perfect bodies, and perfect perfection, we have the platform. It's up there, microphone in hand, that the Christian celebrities allow us a glimpse of spiritual success. It's not a case of standing up and flaunting. The Christian celebrity game plays by more subtle rules, where less is most definitely more: the conspiracy of silence covers a multitude of blemishes, and in part it's the stuff that they leave out that bothers me. Without the honest admission of "I'm failing at this" or "I'm struggling with that," we can believe that success means no struggles at all. The message comes across loud and clear: This is what it takes to be a success. This what you should aim for. This is the spiritual six-pack.

Do It Large

Size matters, baby, and if you're going to do something for God, you're better off making sure it's a noticeable achievement. Keen on evangelism? Aim for the most conversions. After a bit of media recognition? Aim for the national press. Putting on an event? Aim for the biggest audience possible. In the world of the spiritual six-pack, the biggest is always the best.

To the Nations

Keep it glamorous. If we're going to dream of doing great things for God, then we'd best be tied in to the most glitzy and glamorous. Not that we're talking limos and private jets, but perhaps we're not too far behind. A dog-eared, well-stamped passport can tell a story about its Christian owner: They've made it. The best present we can give a baby? Why, the prophecy that he will grow up to fulfill a mighty calling on his life to go to the nations. After all, who wants to be told that their precious newborn is going to be used by God down at the local supermarket? It just doesn't have the same swing, does it? Just like with any Western news agency, we have clear ideas about what is and what isn't newsworthy. Working with the homeless people in New York? Front page stuff. Doing the same in your home town? Turn to page 13.

Follow a Hero (or For the Smallest Minority, Be a Hero Yourself)

The world, so the six-packers tell us, needs role models, and nowhere more so than in the Church. There they are, carving a niche for themselves in the media, dazzling us with their eloquence and wowing us with their downright funkiness. The hero exudes confidence, assurance, charisma, and perfection. All those blemishes and struggles are ignored, leaving us with a clear view of all the positive stuff for us to aim at.

Can That Really Be True?

Is this all going a bit too far? After all, aren't we supposed to press on to reach the prize, to aim higher than our present situation? Of course, but as mentioned already (and will be examined in time) we've somehow got our wires crossed about exactly what the goal itself is.

Before we move on, a word about those six-packers. Are they all like that? Are they all up there busting an ego to get more gold stars? Should we steer clear of all conferences, burn all books, and play Frisbee with the albums? Of course not, and it's probably unhelpful to think about it in terms of individuals. Instead it's a system, a way of doing things that has become an almost-unstoppable snowball. These beliefs that God likes things big, glam, and heroic are so ingrained in the Church that, to some extent, we all buy into it. We all are guilty of misinterpreting the truth, and we all need to step back and take a good look at both the system and the way it has infected our own lives. When I look at mine, it's clear that chasing the six-pack has found a home in me, too; so often I'm tempted to put God in a box, to believe that He only works in certain ways. I'm liable to look up to heroes too, keen to mimic their own success, partial to living my ambition through theirs and forgetting to push on with the calling that God has on my own life. But this is me, and for the rest of us the filters might have delivered another slant of six-packism altogether. From confusing true worship of God with large-scale worship meetings to putting our trust in the hero more than in God, the symptoms are all around us. Whether it's believing that God can only use us if we work in the Church, that preaching is more valuable than serving, or that the Christian life should be free of difficulties, confusions, pain, and grief, these off-center values threaten to take us away from a true relationship with God.

But Doesn't God Do It Large?

Check out the Bible, and it's full of amazing tales of God's mighty power. From floods to fires, huge crowds to the risen dead, the message comes screaming from every page: He is able. And He is. Absolutely. No doubt about it. God is a *can-do* kinda guy. Doing it large is well within His abilities, and His actions are always the result of His heart; He moves because He loves. But if His love for His creation can find expression in the spectacular, it can equally be seen in the small and ordinary.

When the Israelites were busted out of captivity, their miraculous escape was secured by that most inspiring of God-movements—the parting of the Red Sea. But why is the tale there? Is it a bit of flexing and preening by the Lord? Not at all. In fact, when the

Israelites were safely on the other side, there is no report of them saying, "Wow. That really was a HUGE body of water You parted back there, God. Far bigger than any we've seen parted before." Nope. Thank you was far more the order of the day, and God's miracle had a dual purpose. Not only did it save their hides from the Egyptian sword, but it also sparked their faith: "And when the Israelites saw the great power the Lord displayed against the Egyptians, the people feared the Lord and put their trust in him" (Exod. 14:31).

It was no sideshow, no distraction to keep them amused while the journey dragged by. It was a practical solution to a couple of problems: their imminent annihilation and their lack of understanding of the character of their God. There is an agenda behind the works of God, one which we can sometimes forget when we get caught up in our size-matters faith. God's tools come in varying shapes and sizes, and they always are used for a purpose. We would do well to remember we walk a fine line between believing on one side that big is always God's best and on the other side that God's best is sometimes big.

But Doesn't God Change Lives?

I grew up thinking that men of God married babes. I had put a lot of energy into researching this—mostly I spent time staring at good looking older women—and my conclusions helped spur me on to read the Bible every day for at least a month. I was utterly convinced that not only would my future wife be a total honey, but that the rest of my life would be similarly peachy as well. And in part I'd stumbled across something right: God is in the business of changing lives. But this particular truth comes prepacked with a side order of confusion. Sometimes those changed lives look very nice, thank you very much, and it can be frighteningly easy to assume that with God in my life I'm bound to get the job, the house, and the partner that I want. It's only a short jump from there to believing that God will always make our lives a "success." Whatever we want to do—goes the logic—God will bless it and make it God. With Him on our side, everything has potential, every aspect of our lives can be a soar-away success.

But the cross tells a slightly different story, or at least it adds another paragraph. God does change lives, but it's a question of framework. While we may scrabble around wondering about *our* ambitions for *our* lives during the next year or so, looking for the fruits of success to be ready to eat this season, we forget that God sees a much wider picture. The fruits of success are not there primarily for our enjoyment but for His glory. The message of the cross underlines the fact that even death itself is not failure. Church history is littered with examples of the Christian imperative to desire more than just a cushy life, and while we might laugh at the idea that God makes all Christians rich as long as they believe in Him enough, we can still fall prey to the line that coming to Jesus means that He will wipe away all our tears. Instead of kissing them all away, Jesus offers a new perspective: Suffering is not a sign of failure.

But Wasn't Jesus a Hero?

Yes, indeed, and this profound truth should be enough to calm all our strutting and remind us of what the score really is. Jesus is the hero, not us. We're called to follow Him, but not to be Him: Christianity is not a fast-food franchise where we sign up, collect the starter pack, don the uniform, and set about recreating the original in a way that hopes no one will notice the difference. Why? Because people will notice the difference. It may come as a shock, but there's actually a bit of a gap between Jesus' standards and our own lifestyles. All it takes is a quick look over my own life to confirm the truth of that statement. I'm a mush of rusted passion, poisoned motives, and gangrenous attitudes. Believe me, if you knew what was really in my head you'd ... well, let's just say I could do better, OK? We're all struggling with sin, all failing to match up to God's standards. So let's not allow our egos to get in the way. He's the one we're all following, and sometimes our desire to be at the front of the pack can make it difficult for others to get a clear view of the leader. 'Nuff said.

The Danger of Unwanted Side Effects

With our bodies pressed into the six-pack workout program, we run the risk of encountering some unpleasant side effects in the form of a whole bunch of confusing messages about Christianity. Sadly, almost everyone is affected, from the ones showing off their toned physiques to the wannabe six-packers just starting out. The results, well ... we'll get to those.

I used to play guitar for a guy at church. For three or four years the band would get invited to various events to help him lead the worship. They were good times, and I probably still miss them a little, but there are sides of the whole thing that I hope never to see again. As time went by and we became slightly less appalling on our instruments, we got invited along to play at larger events. After a while we were allowed to share the bill with other bands and speakers, and it was an honor and a pleasure to meet them. But there was one event that changed it all for me.

It was the biggest one we'd ever been along to, and probably the biggest one anyone else involved had been a part of, too. There was a lot of chat about it for the months building up, and on the day many people turned up at Wembley Stadium to worship God and hear some teaching. But there was a side to it that somehow turned me—and many others—off. The dressing rooms were full of people stressing about how well or poorly their solos had gone. The costume changes were precise, well thought-out, and designed to make the wearers look their very best from the stage. It was a turnoff to say the least, and the backstage attitudes—the "I can't believe I'm getting to play in front of so many people"—made it all a bit hard to swallow. Especially as I'd had my hair cut for it. I, too, had made moves in the same direction, and was only pulled back by the sight of our keyboard player dropping a criminally overloaded plate of full English breakfast onto his lap. He'd brought nothing with him in the way of a costume change and was forced to appear in front of the masses with an egg-stained crotch. It was kind of hard to take things seriously after that.

These events, these wholesale six-pack outlets where we are encouraged to come along and learn from the platform, can be mixed. Of course, there is so much good to be said for Christians gathering together to worship God, to pray, to get inspired, and to be reminded of the need for unity. But there is a danger that those on the platform believe the hype a little too much. Their presence on the stage is no more a sign of spiritual success than the quality of their costumes. There can be a pressure on such people to keep up appearances, to exhibit the correct signals when, in reality, life is very different altogether.

But let's not get stuck on this. There are other side effects of the six-pack workout, and not just ones that can be seen on the "instructors." The messages we hear lead us in a wrong direction, and the consequences are not hard to second-guess. We hear talk of "remarkable families," of people who have been through so much and on whom God has an almighty calling. For that message we may sometimes read "others are worth more than me." At times we might hear about people feeling happy about an opportunity to "go for the big one," to take a step further toward recognition. My wife used to do a bit of dancing on stage at events and was once asked after a meeting by someone how they should go about using their dancing skills in worship. It so happens that Emma (Mrs. Borlase) had seen them giving all they had during the worship, and she told them that they already were using their skills. "No, no," came the reply. "I mean dancing in worship so that God can use me," she said pointing at the stage. The lesson about success being in front of people had clearly been well studied.

Of course, for some the realization that there is a hierarchy of Christian service is too much, and they leave altogether. I've known people who have left church altogether because of feeling left out, and I'm convinced that most of us will go through some point in our lives when we feel frustrated that our gifts are not recognized nor our talents used. And just in the same way that the constant billboard-barrage telling us that slim = beautiful seeps down deep into our subconscious and infects almost our entire view of our bodies, so too does the misbelief that God prefers us famous throw us offtrack.

Dissatisfaction, Disappointment, and Defeat

We can easily end up dissatisfied with our lot. The gifts we have may not match up with the ones that seem to be so visible in the six-packers. We might not be musical, confident in front of a crowd, or able to pray eloquently and at length, and we're led to the conclusion that the talents we do have will mark us out for a second-rate relationship with God. This adopted ambition, this fool's gold, leaves us forever hungry and never satisfied. How unlike a true relationship with God does that sound?

At times I have felt like a disappointment to God, that in some way I have let Him down. Surely He loves the people up front far more than me, so the logic goes. After all, they seem to be enjoying themselves so much more than I am, so they must be making Him happier, too. And, of course, it does often seem that way, as another roll of laughter falls out of their immaculately dentured mouths or another story of victory lashes the deck. It's as if they're sharing a private joke with the Almighty, enjoying a quiet gin and tonic with Him on the terrace before dinner. We, on the other hand, are left going over the same old question: Could God like me? "Not like this," comes the answer.

And, of course, we can all feel defeated. Not only have we failed God and in some way been failed by Him, but we can also hook up with the idea that we are minor players. We are inconsequential, of little importance to the grand scheme of things. The big events are the tokens; they are the place at which things really happen. Our lives are of little importance, and we give up on ever trying to make a difference in and with them. After all, it makes sense, doesn't it? The others are better at doing the important stuff, so why not leave it all up to them? They never seem to fail, and the results are always so much more spectacular whenever they move into gear; wouldn't it be a waste of resources to try to copy them? But this view leads us to deny all responsibility for our own lives. We let the leaders lead, the teachers tell us what to think, and the evangelists pull in the souls for the kingdom. It's called outsourcing, and really, it makes life so much easier. I feel gutted that I wasted years chasing after the wrong goal altogether. Actually, "chasing" makes it sound like too active a pursuit, and it's probably far more accurate to describe much of my early Christian walk as a "slouch." I was a firm—if not exactly conscious—believer that it was more important to go along to an event than to work on my lifestyle. Evangelism was more about clinching the deal with a prayer of repentance than discipling friends. Worship was about singing the notes right, playing the tunes well, and making sure it looked and sounded right. As for the heart behind it all ... let's just say it needed some surgery.

Copying the Culture

In signing up for a version of the faith that places tokenistic events over real-life changes, the Church drops a few hints about which influences are at work. During the last thirty years or so, much has been said about the decline in church attendance. But on closer inspection it appears that this does not apply to all churches; instead, many of the fired-up and feisty charismatic churches have experienced actual growth. It's just that with so many "dead" churches finally kicking the bucket, it seems that all around is falling.

And it is in the renewed part of the Church that much of this six-packism is taking place. I can remember growing up in a church that followed the Anglican order of service, with a good strong structure underpinning every service. Years later, the same church is still going strong and, like many others, has ditched the formal order of service in favor of a much more open and spontaneous meeting. In each service there will be some worship, preaching, and time for prayer, but the vibe is very much more "anything goes" than it used to be way back in the late '70s. So much good has come along with this change, but parceled up with it has been a pressure on those leading the meeting to entertain. After all, if people aren't given a book to lead them, then they need another way of keeping their minds focused on the job at hand. And so the services have become entertaining, with good gags, charismatic preachers, and attention-grabbing worship.

Remind you of anything? It's just like the culture that exists on the other side of the vestry. Our desire to be entertained—be it by the National Lottery, the latest pop idol, or a decent dose of political scandal—is a driving force behind many a money-making venture. Shopping malls cater to the whole "shopping experience"; politicians have personality; soap stars want to get into pop; and *www.yourmobile.com* will give you almost any song you want as a ring tone. And it's free. So that's nice. The Church suffers under the pressure to do likewise (entertain, not provide free ring tones), and before long, the service becomes more about keeping bums on seats than it is about keeping eyes on God.

The residue flavors of materialism and "I want it now" can also be recognized in the communion wine. There is a pressure for the church service to provide an instant high, a money-back-if-not-fully-satisfied guarantee that this thing works, and all you have to do is stroll in, make your selection, and clip, strap, or stick it on to your life. But forget the question about whether it's right to suggest that finding God is as easy as ordering a supersized super value meal, what about whether it's possible at all? Sure salvation is free and open to all, but are we really wise to let people believe that relationship with God is a matter of plug and play?

Recently we've seen the rise of the instant celebrity. Turn on your TV, and you're bound to see a docu-soap, a real-life drama, some program about DIY for novices presented by novices. At the time of writing, television audiences are glued to *Big Brother*, a regular perv-fest which seems to be the ultimate in what they're now calling celibritocity: the cult of easy recognition. There was a time when people streaked at sports events for a bit of attention, but now a wannabe faces far more options: Do I join a manufactured pop band, call *Trading Spaces*, or stalk Tom Cruise? Oh, the agony of choice.

What's this got to do with the Church? Like it or not, we're signing up for the same. We have Christian versions of anything from pop stars to business tycoons, and we're bound into the spirit of the age. The only trouble—well, not the only trouble—is that in the Christian subculture it comes off all "big fish in a small pond," which, all things considered, is a bit of a shame.

Six-Packers of the Past

The desire to make monuments to our own greatness is nothing new, unfortunately. Just take a look at the story of Noah. The story kicks off in Genesis 6 with a clear description of the state of the world. The verdict? A definite thumbs-down. Not only is there intermarriage between separate groups, but a messed-up hero system:

> The Nephilim were on the earth in those days—and also afterward—when the sons of God went to the daughters of men and had children by them. They were the heroes of old, men of renown. The Lord saw how great man's wickedness on the earth had become, and that every inclination of the thoughts of his heart was only evil all the time. The Lord was grieved that he had made man on the earth, and his heart was filled with pain. So the Lord said, "I will wipe mankind, whom I have created, from the face of the earth—men and animals, and creatures that move along the ground, and birds of the air—for I am grieved that I have made them." (Gen. 6:4-7)

The Nephilim were big strong lads, and in men's eyes they were the heroes. In God's eyes things were a little different, and the Hebrew word *nephilim* means "fallen ones." And it seems that the heroes hadn't done a good job in the way of leading the people. Of course, we're supposed to sit up when we read the line about

God grieving; there's something seriously wrong when we do the sinning and God does the repenting, don't you think?

What follows is a familiar story: Noah is the only decent egg out of the whole pack, and God uses him to move humanity into the next phase. Humanity may not be able to escape the consequences of its sin, but Noah's story—like Adam and Eve's—shows us that life has certain responsibilities that go with it. Adam and Eve had to obey God's commands, and Noah's contemporaries refused. The picture emerges: living away from God has certain consequences. But there's a characteristic of God that we must be careful not to overlook: salvation, and it goes alongside His judgment.

> Noah, a man of the soil, proceeded to plant a vineyard. When he drank some of its wine, he became drunk and lay uncovered inside his tent. Ham, the father of Canaan, saw his father's nakedness and told his two brothers outside. But Shem and Japheth took a garment and laid it across their shoulders; then they walked in backward and covered their father's nakedness. Their faces were turned the other way so that they would not see their father's nakedness. (Gen. 9:20-23)

After the flood is over, after the waters have subsided and the animals offloaded, Noah grows a few vines and gets wasted on home-brew. Oh dear. Not really the stuff of heroes now, is it? How, I wonder, did that little episode creep into the manuscript? Surely some mistake? But perhaps not, perhaps we hold Noah too highly if we assume that his drunkenness made him a poor choice. You see, God used Noah despite his weakness. It wasn't something that needed to be swept under the carpet, a little secret that was best left untold. If we believe that our heroes are free of weakness, then we find ourselves in the minefield of believing that the works God does through them have anything to do with them in the first place. Yes, Noah trusted and was faithful to God in the midst of massive opposition, but the miracle of the flood was all God's work. The Nephilim were no good as heroes and role models, and Noah's example comes a distant second to the love, judgment, and mercy of God Himself. It's all about focus.

God had blessed Noah, telling him to get on with the job of establishing a large family of descendants. Another chapter goes by, and we see that just that has happened with sons being born and the numbers increasing. Yet the script seems remarkably familiar; by the time chapter 11 kicks off, we see mankind back to its old tricks again of moving the focus away from God.

> Now the whole world had one language and a common speech. As men moved eastward, they found a plain in Shinar and settled there. They said to each other, "Come, let's make bricks and bake them thoroughly." They used brick instead of stone, and tar for mortar. Then they said, "Come, let us build ourselves a city, with a tower that reaches to the heavens, so that we may make a name for ourselves and not be scattered over the face of the whole earth." But the Lord came down to see the city and the tower that the men were building. The Lord said, "If as one people speaking the same language they have begun to do this, then nothing they plan to do will be impossible for them. Come, let us go down and confuse their language so they will not understand each other." So the Lord scattered them from there over all the earth, and they stopped building the city. That is why it was called

Babel—because there the Lord confused the language of the whole world. From there the Lord scattered them over the face of the whole earth. (Gen. 11:1-9)

It's the same old story: wandering away from God but unable to avoid the consequences of sin. This time it's the desire to make a name for themselves that has caught their attention, and the aim of doing something impressive, something remarkable that will wow others is simply not on target. Just check out the arrogant tone of the language in verse 4: "us ... ourselves ... we ... ourselves." There's a clear agenda that's been set by the people, but the pathetic nature of their achievements is highlighted by the writer when he suggests that God had to descend in order to view this stunted tower.

This is not a warm-up to some old-time fire-and-brimstone rant about the need for God to annihilate every last one of us. Instead it strikes me that things have changed remarkably little since these stories were written. We struggle with God, trying to keep the glories for ourselves, no matter what those glories might be. The blessing of increased population left the crew at Shinar puffed up with pride, while the ticket receipts from a well-attended meeting might leave us feeling similarly impressed. What's more, we are all bearers of weaknesses. We all walk with a limp, even though we do such a good job of trying to hide it. Of course, our mistakes are embarrassing, but in hiding them are we guilty of presenting ourselves in too good a light?

The Real Godly Success

Surprising as it may seem, I don't think God is all that fussed about our physique. Whether the six-pack is spiritual or physical, I think the reaction would be far more "that's nice, dear" than "wow!" God's idea of success is something else altogether.

A quick glance through the Bible will turn up some common themes. Look at Samuel, Abraham and Sarah, David, Joseph, Elisha, Mary, and Jesus—to name but a few—and you'll see that each of them went through long periods of what looked like inactivity before they finally kicked into the big time of carrying out God's public purpose for their lives. Why? It's all about the character. God doesn't need a selection of the most talented individuals to run things for Him while He's out of town for a few millennia; instead, He's after character to follow through with the calling even when things don't look so great.

If you're after a tasty example, we'll settle down at Job. OK, so there's all that weird stuff at the beginning where Satan's strolling about the garden laying down bets with God. It's all too weird for me, but I'm comforted by the fact that many other cultures have a Job story: one of testing and perseverance.

First he gets hit by four intense body blows: Arabs, lightning, Chaldeans, and a tornado all move into town and rough him up just a little. It's strong stuff, but the man hangs in there despite the fact that his wealth and family are gone. The sores over his body are a different story, however, but even though he has shaved his head and cut himself to relieve the pain, he stays clear of sin. He may look different, but the heart is still the same.

As the story moves on, we read of the three friends who first come and sit with him in silence, and then offer advice as to why Job's life seems to have turned a deeper shade of pain. Is he in denial? Is it due to sin? Is it actually not that bad considering what he *really* deserves? No, no, and no is the answer: Suffering does not necessarily indicate the presence of sin. And if that's the case, what is it for anyway?

In steps young Elihu, the fourth and most sensible of the friends.

> But I tell you, in this you are not right, for God is greater
> than man. Why do you complain to him that he answers
> none of man's words? For God does speak—now one
> way, now another—though man may not perceive it. In a
> dream, in a vision of the night, when deep sleep falls on
> men as they slumber in their beds, he may speak in their
> ears and terrify them with warnings, to turn man from
> wrongdoing and keep him from pride, to preserve his
> soul from the pit, his life from perishing by the sword.
> (Job 33:12-18)

God is the teacher, using suffering as a path toward greater wisdom. At the end, God speaks: "Brace yourself like a man," Job is told, perhaps catching us off our guard. The original word used for *man* does not imply a weak man—kind of as you'd expect for one standing in front of God—but a strong one, one ready to fight:

> Where were you when I laid the earth's foundation? Tell
> me, if you understand. Who marked off its dimensions?
> Surely you know! Who stretched a measuring line across
> it? On what were its footings set, or who laid its corner-
> stone—while the morning stars sang together and all the
> angels shouted for joy? Who shut up the sea behind doors
> when it burst forth from the womb? (Job 38:4-8)

God asks him questions, the sort none of us could answer. Job does no better than us, but standing face to face, hearing of all that God has done, recognizing once again his place in the universe, Job bows down and worships (42:6). He is restored, and while the three wise monkeys get a telling off, Job is held up as a righteous man.

Is Job a far-out example, one of no real relevance to us today? He might get dragged out to shove under the nose of the grieving relative, but the story has plenty to say to us even now. For many of us it is precisely at the point where things start to get difficult that we begin to question just how much the spiritual six-pack helps us. And, of course, it's not that much good in itself. Job was doing very nicely, thank you very much, as the prologue makes clear:

> In the land of Uz there lived a man whose name was Job. This man was blameless and upright; he feared God and shunned evil. He had seven sons and three daughters, and he owned seven thousand sheep, three thousand camels, five hundred yoke of oxen and five hundred donkeys, and had a large number of servants. He was the greatest man among all the people of the East. (Job 1:1-3)

He was doing it large, taking it to the nations, and being a hero, but in just a handful of verses it had all been stripped away, pruned back to allow us to see the heart behind it all. And what did we see? Obedience, sacrifice, and relationship—the real twinkles in God's eye.

Mirror Image

Here I am back in front of the mirror. Still naked, a little tired after having looked so closely at the way things really are for me. I've come up with some conclusions too: like this life is more about coping with things that are difficult than manufacturing things so that life is easy. The aim of the game is not to make it into a shiny limo, to speed away from hardship without a care in the world. As a person who works with drug addicts once said of the events in the church in Toronto: "When we heard that people were catching the plane to go to the place where the laughing was, we didn't understand. But we though that if this was God it wouldn't be long before they caught the plane to come to the place where the crying was too. We waited. You didn't come."

I heard about an ambition recently. "I want to live a quiet life. To know God, to love him, to serve and follow." That was it. No specifics, no action plan for saving the world. Nothing that would make it into the news. But it struck me as something wonderful, a healthy body image, an ambition that was built to last. This is not a call to ditch the dreams of doing things for God, not a suggestion that we give up following Him or taking brave steps to take the Gospel message out. But it is a question mark over just how we think God does use us. Of course, part of the six-pack's nature is that it is defined and pert. It's also pretty small and easily hidden. Are we so sure that God only works through people on the stage, in the public eye, and without failings? Isn't there so much more to Him than that?

A final word in front of the mirror. Giving up on the six-pack is a tricky business, not in the least because the alternatives are so hard to define. If living a good life for God involves obedience, sacrifice, and relationship, then we're going to have to change our attitude. The six-pack can be achieved; we may be tempted to believe that one day we will arrive and claim that we've "made it"; but true godly success comes with no absolutes, no finishing post. After all, can we ever be obedient enough, sacrificial enough, or close enough to God? Job had to sit through thirty-eight chapters of God's silence before he heard Him speak, and even then there was no explanation for what went on. How long could we last?

"The shape of the Church will change as people begin to get a better perspective on the way things have been going."

2

Why Do I Want to Look Like This?

Watering Hole Christianity

A couple of days ago, I was coming home from a night out with some old friends. There were just two of us left on the train traveling out to the provinces, and Andy and I were catching up, having not seen each other for a few months.

"Don't you ever think," he asked as his stop approached, "that one day you'll look back and say, 'I remember when I was a born-again Christian'?"

My first reaction stayed around for a while. "Of course not," I told him. This was for life. Relationship. Love. New life. Salvation. I started blabbing on about how great God is, how Jesus turned things upside down, how there's an edge to Christianity that is profoundly political, far more challenging and exciting than the "me first" attitude that screams down from the billboards and magazine back covers. I was still going when he got off the train. I think he's used to me getting a little excited from time to time, and he probably said it to wind me up.

Moving on, my thoughts took a sharp turn away from "I'll always be a born-again Christian" to "What is this 'born-again' thing after all?" It struck me as a strange phrase, and I wondered where he'd picked it up from. It has been a long time since I used it, and while my first reaction was to jump in and stake my claim, with a bit of reflection I began to wonder; the phrase was big a couple of decades back, but does it really have the zing and sparkle today? Surely it belongs back in the box along with Reactolite sunglasses, tank tops, and John Denver. Maybe it's just the niche I'm involved in, but it's been ages since I heard anyone describe oneself as being born again. My fellow niche-dwellers and I have grown so big in number that it's almost taken for granted that these days a new Christian will be one brought into the charismatic side of things, introduced to the Holy Spirit, and encouraged to get to know Him as soon as possible. And all the better for it, I say.

But if born again was a badge to be worn, one that made it clear that you were part of something new, a sub-group of the faith which felt itself on the cutting edge, then where are we now? Revived-again Christians? Remixed Christians? Post-evangelical Christians? What does it matter anyway? After all, the box, the label, don't they just take us away from the real deal: that we are Christians, plain and simple? Why do we feel this need to add on, subdivide, classify, and adopt as a shiny new badge?

Yet, it's not that long ago that I was desperate to call myself more than just a Christian. That was far too vague a title, one that could have included anyone from a cobwebbed octogenarian Vicar in Stowe-on-the-Wolde to a woolly liberal worshiping God through a cheese slice in Clapham. No, that simply wouldn't do. I needed something else, something to really capture the sense of zeal that sent out a glow all day long. What I needed to be called was something else altogether—an on-fire Christian.

My flames burned bright every night of the week. How could you tell? Because I was at church. Somehow I got it into my mind that what mattered most during the autumn of my final year at university was being surrounded by Christians. I needed to keep safe, warm, and topped up with as much high-grade spiritual gas as was humanly possible. I went to church on Sunday, naturally, but not just once. Not just twice either, as that miserable downtime between 12:30 and 6:00 p.m. managed to get filled with extra prayer meetings, band practices, and plenty of lingering about before and after each service. On Tuesday and Thursday there were meetings to prepare for the Friday night worship gig, while Wednesday was the midweek home-group meeting. Saturday was spent out with church friends and getting excited about the following day. All that was left was Monday. I hated Mondays. Cold sweats and that uncomfortable feeling in the pit of my stomach all day. I winced all the way through it, desperate to get it over with and move on to the safety of the next day's meetings. How come? I was scared. To me, any time spent out of church was time spent in the dangerous wilderness called The World. I was at risk of spiritual contamination, terrorism, kidnapping, and all-around infection. Sudden noises made me jump, and my cross was never far from my side. The fear had me gripped, and for almost eight weeks I lived by a simple mantra: church is safe, world is bad.

The Watering Hole

There's a theory doing the rounds that the Church is like a watering hole—one of those welcome natural sources of water out in the desert that feeds a huge variety of natural life. Here's the deal: We are the animals, the Church is the hole. We depend on the hole for the source of life itself, and without it we're stuffed. Like a real watering hole, things can get a little crowded, and there's a pecking order about who gets to be in the prime spots at the water's edge. What's more, the fittest and strongest will fight their way toward those prime spots while the weak ones will hang around the edges. It's there that they find themselves an easy target for the wild predators, and many of them get attacked and carried off. If only they'd spent more time at the center of the action, they would never have been in the position to get picked off in the first place.

I'm not a fan of the analogy. Correction, I'm a fan of the analogy, but I'm not a fan of the reality. The trouble is that, for many of us, it does describe pretty accurately the attitude that we have to church, or the attitude that the Church has to us: that the aim is to spend as much time as possible there, and that those on the edge, those who find it difficult, are bound to get picked on, beaten up, and turned over by all the nasty beasties out there in the big, bad world. And the real problem I have with it is this: It just doesn't match up with the model shown in the Bible. It just doesn't make sense. For all my desperate attempts to fill my life with nothing but church, the fear only made me a weaker Christian. I lost sight of the true nature of God and put my faith in superstitious ritual and lifestyle-free obligations.

The idea that Christianity is all about a life lived within the walls of the Church is closely linked in with much of that six-pack stuff. It's the source of much of our confusion because of a simple fact: If we only teach that Christianity is best lived within the Church, then we believe that Christianity works best within the Church. It's a short step from "be here now" to "platform = wow."

Of course, for many of us, the picture of extreme church attendance, of free-flowing paranoia, just doesn't wash. We've got the whole thing sussed, we tell ourselves, combining the life on the inside of the Church with the life on the outside. But I wonder if it really is as open and shut a case as that. Is church really only about the meetings? Do we have a clear view of just how much we can integrate the spiritual gifts with worldly interaction? Is Christianity really about making choices between time in church and time out of it?

But this isn't a buildup to some free-wheeling rant about why I'm offended by the Church, why my bags are packed, and I'm pausing just long enough to shout something cutting before the slammed door confirms my exit. This is simply how this naked Christian feels: confused mainly, but chewing the pen-top of faith and wondering about things. Whether we struggle to keep our interest up at church or find that it's our most favorite place to be, it's important to step back and ask ourselves the serious questions: What is the subconscious message being put across? How does it affect the congregation? How close have we come to fulfilling our potential?

Life at the Watering Hole

It certainly does seem that many of the "strongest" Christians I know are at the water's edge. Many of these lovely, godly people—who do a great job in encouraging others to move closer to God—feel strangely dissatisfied that their lives are so surrounded by this distorted view of how church should run.

"The only time I talk to non-Christians," said one of them a few years back, "is when I buy a paper."

Of course, the Church is made up of different people with different gifts—some pastors, some evangelists and so on as Paul mentions in Ephesians 4—and in our diversity the sum is greater than the parts, but it can prove awkward. Gideon was told to wheedle out the soldiers from his army who drank from the river "like dogs," putting their faces in the water and lapping it up. Those who cupped their hands to their mouth were allowed to stay, the implication being that they were far wiser soldiers, remaining aware that a surprise attack may take place. Those left lapping were far more vulnerable and considered a liability. So should we sack the pastor? Ditch the deacon? Not at all, but perhaps this image of the soldiers can be helpful. When we focus on nothing other than the water in front of us, when we forget the context in which we find ourselves, we become far less useful in the fight. OK, so the fight imagery might be a bit too hardcore, but in terms of pure focus it raises the point that seeing the world so narrowly might cause problems.

These extremes might help illustrate a point, but for most, church life will be played out somewhere between the two. It is here where the real battle is fought, with the struggle to maintain a faith that works in the world on one side squaring up to the pressures of a model that seems best applied within the walls of the Church. For these people, the watering hole does not so much describe their attitude, but the model they are offered. And like the animals in the original picture, they take what they can get. But their silence does not cancel out the imperfections.

However we feel about the watering hole way of doing church, whether we're lapping it up at the water's edge, feeling frustrated on the peripheries, or feeling ambivalent somewhere in between, there's a clear message that comes across. Let me explain. We like meetings. Lots of them. A successful church will, for some of us, have to have successful meetings. We like to fill them with fired-up worship, inspirational talks, life-changing ministry. We want more than just gatherings: we want meetings with God, times that we will be able to look back on and say "we moved on with God through them." There's a pressure on the leaders and congregation to have an "encounter" with God every time we get together, and because of this our view of the Church can become narrow. *What does the Church do?* we ask ourselves. Have meetings. *How does it change lives?* Through the meetings. *How do we show how God works?* In the meetings. *Where do we use our talents?* You get the picture.

More Than Just Meetings

There's a church I heard of once that seemed to be pretty successful. Here's the story:

Things kicked off with a massive encounter with the Holy Spirit. It was like nothing they'd ever experienced before, and it changed things forever. Suddenly they knew that the power of God was at work in their lives, and Peter—one of the founders—preached an absolute diamond of a sermon to the crowd of people who had gathered to watch. After that the church seemed to multiply like cells, with each day that passed bringing new people along to be a part of things. People got to hear about them from their involvement with the community—healing the sick and helping the poor. They were a radical bunch, but their activities did not go unnoticed by the people with the power to kick up a bit of a fuss. Soon there were beatings, imprisonments, and even death, but not for the pasty-looking wastrels on the fringe of things, but some of their most committed individuals. The inevitable internal squabbles and politics took their toll too, and as things eventually got just a little too heavy, the crew split, taking their ballistic message with them wherever they went.

A new boy came along, one with a bit of a shifty past, but the salvation of the sinner was well within God's grasp. At the same time there was a change of gear as Peter realized that where they had been previously aiming their message at one group of people, the Gospel message was, in fact, relevant for all, regardless of race, history, or background. Things went a bit nutty as this real-ization acted like a mainline steroid buzz, increasing the spread and activity of the Church in all areas.

More death and persecution followed, but still the Church at large remained strong in its aim to reach out. It went from country to country, tackling the tough issues that created a false idea of hierarchy within the Church. More countries were visited, more trouble encountered, and more people introduced to the life-changing love of God.

OK, so we can't all expect to be part of something so dramatic, but these first three decades in the history of the Church show a side that we may perhaps have forgotten. The life of the Church was found in the believers, and it was their actions that led to the spread. The meetings were a vital part of learning, of sharing, and of worshiping. They were also the launch pad from which the believers obeyed the command of Matthew 28:19—"go." With this attitude in place, the believers' activities took on a dif-ferent texture and tone, with Luke describing their early actions like this:

> They devoted themselves to the apostles' teaching and
> to the fellowship, to the breaking of bread and to prayer.
> Everyone was filled with awe, and many wonders and
> miraculous signs were done by the apostles. All the
> believers were together and had everything in common.
> Selling their possessions and goods, they gave to anyone
> as he had need. Every day they continued to meet togeth-
> er in the temple courts. They broke bread in their homes
> and ate together with glad and sincere hearts, praising

God and enjoying the favor of all the people. And the
Lord added to their number daily those who were being
saved. (Acts 2:42-47)

The meetings were not the entire life of the Church. Instead,
they were a tool with which to sculpt the life of the believers. Of
course, church meetings are not wrong, but when they become
our focus, when the aim is to make them the work of art in themselves, we find ourselves in dangerous water.

A friend told me about a church he had been a part of. It was busy,
time-consuming stuff, and being a member took up pretty much
every spare bit of time and energy that he had. There was great
teaching, prayer meetings, outreach events, social action projects,
and a whole side of pastoral work that pulled the people together.
For my friend and many others, it was a wonderful experience.
"Church as it was meant to be," she called it. "And it took up your
whole life."

I recoiled. Church taking up more than a couple of hours on
Sunday and a midweek evening? You must be joking. Church,
in my mind, was there to serve, to support me in the rest of the
work that I did outside. Slotting other engagements around it was
a sign of failure, a clear indication that I was missing the balance
between fellowship and action. After all, I thought, who wants to
be a part of the Christian ghetto?

But I hadn't been listening, and she described the life of the
church in greater detail. It was not church as a retreat, but church
as a vibrant community. It was not so much a static event as an
organic body. Yes, there was teaching, but there were the outlets
for the application, too. This was no desert watering hole; this

was a river flowing through a city, one where it wasn't just the members that benefited. How different from an isolated event, a place that is isolated from the rest of life. This is not about encouraging us all to sign up for endless church-based activities, but instead a question mark over just how fresh the water is in the hole. Is Christianity really supposed to be a faith lived out in isolation? Is it really supposed to be carried out behind closed doors? Is the main aim of church to encourage people to be better at attending meetings?

In the summer of 2000 something odd happened; ten thousand young Christians went up to Manchester to spend time living life out loud. The days kicked off with worship in song at a big meeting, and straight after they went out onto the street to run cafés, meet people, and—most surprisingly for many of the residents—work for free. They cleaned up playgrounds, painted houses, did the gardening, and performed loads of other good and kind acts. This was church without walls, church plus, church as it was supposed to be, combining the lifeblood of worshiping, giving, learning, and receiving from God together within the meeting with the same lifeblood outside the meetings. This is my church, so the song goes. And I'm so proud to be a part of it.

How Much Water Do We Need?

My wife went through a difficult point in her life, leaving college early on and feeling weighed down by the pressure of extreme stress. "I was wounded," she says. "I was like a child again, and I just needed to be held." Family and friends were there for her, as was church. It was so important for her to be able to feel that she could turn up as often as she wanted and relax in the safety of church. She went to every meeting, sometimes going up for prayer at every opportunity, while at other times she'd just sit back and soak it all in. Being surrounded by Christians reminded her of the truth about God, about His love and power. For a long time, the church meetings were the strong arms of a nursing mother, holding her tightly, reminding her that things were OK, telling her that here she was safe.

Being at the water's edge is so important. The Church has a vital role to fulfill as hospital, building us up in a safe environment. But for all of us—at whatever stage of the rehab process we're at—there comes a point when the confidence comes back, the healing kicks in, and we feel ready again to take up Jesus' command to "go." That doesn't mean that we leave, and it doesn't mean that we never return for regular checkups, top-offs, and therapy. But we must allow ourselves to move around within the full breadth of church. Recuperating, refuelling, repairing, preparing, and engaging, these are all functions within the body.

What Does the Water Taste Like?

Take any church virgin off the street and plonk him down in the back row at a regular church service, and the chances are that he'll feel just a tad confused. Forget the fact that the only other similar experience of sitting in rows, facing the front, and listening to a preacher would have been his time spent at school, the language, structure, and activity itself would have him scratching his head in confusion. And while to some extent this is to be expected, I wonder whether it really is something to be celebrated. After all, if we only know how to do the Christian things like prophesying, healing, and "ministering to God" while the congregation is gathered in church, it's rather bad news when those activities make little sense to the people who need them most.

Take prophecy, for example. How vital and essential and amazing an idea is that? Hearing God speak? Yes, please. But with the church service being the forum in which prophecy is modeled, we wind up with something that might perhaps be slightly removed from the ideal. Perhaps we might get in the habit of considering prophecy as something mainly for us, for the collective gathered in front of the altar. We may have gotten the idea that prophecy is less about a way of life and more about a spoken word. At the extreme, we might have taken on board the idea that prophecy is a spectator sport, that only those who have "the gift" need bother listening. The rest of us auditorily impaired ones can just sit back and let the others get on with it.

And does it have to be this way? Does God only want to whisper pleasantries in the ears of those already in the know? Look at Elisha, an Old Testament man with a mighty gift for hearing what God had to say to people. Elijah's work was helping to turn the wandering hearts of the Israelites back to God, and some years before he hung up his boots, he selected Elisha as the next man who was to run with the baton. After being selected and having Elijah's cloak placed on him in an act symbolic of the passing on of the work Elijah had begun, there is a ten-year silence on the Elisha front. We hear nothing from him and are left wondering what's going on.

He comes back on the scene as we wave Elijah off, and straight-away the story kicks off with the following:

> The men of the city said to Elisha, "Look, our lord, this town is well situated, as you can see, but the water is bad and the land is unproductive." "Bring me a new bowl," he said, "and put salt in it." So they brought it to him. Then he went out to the spring and threw the salt into it, saying, "This is what the Lord says: 'I have healed this water. Never again will it cause death or make the land

unproductive.'" And the water has remained wholesome to this day, according to the word Elisha had spoken. (2 Kings 2:19-22)

While it's tempting to get all excited about Elisha cleansing the water what with this chapter's chosen metaphor, I think it's safer to stick to the facts. The city—Jericho (see verse 18 if you're keen)—had poisoned water, causing—allegedly—miscarriages. This all ties with the proclamation made by Joshua back in Joshua 6:26 that anyone who rebuilt the city would suffer the curse of infant death. Yet despite this deserved judgment, God has compassion on the people and uses Elisha to heal the water. If we were in any doubt that it was God's miracle, then look again at the method of making it healthy: He puts salt in it. God may work through the obscure and even the mundane, but always for His glory and because of His character.

After a slightly sketchy scene where Elisha loses his rag with some cheeky young kids, we see another tale of the prophetic in action in chapter 4.

> The wife of a man from the company of the prophets cried out to Elisha, "Your servant my husband is dead, and you know that he revered the Lord. But now his creditor is coming to take my two boys as his slaves." Elisha replied to her, "How can I help you? Tell me, what do you have in your house?" "Your servant has nothing there at all," she said, "except a little oil." Elisha said, "Go around and ask all your neighbors for empty jars. Don't ask for just a few. Then go inside and shut the door behind you and your sons. Pour oil into all the jars, and as each is filled, put it to one side." She left him and

afterward shut the door behind her and her sons. They brought the jars to her and she kept pouring. When all the jars were full, she said to her son, "Bring me another one." But he replied, "There is not a jar left." Then the oil stopped flowing. She went and told the man of God, and he said, "Go, sell the oil and pay your debts. You and your sons can live on what is left." (2 Kings 4:1-7)

Along with speaking God's Word comes doing God's work, and as with the healing of the water, this story underlines in bold the fact that God's work includes putting right the wrongs caused by humankind. Here the woman in question had been married to one of the crew of prophets, a decent bunch who make up the subplot of the Elisha saga. It is suggested that this man may have borrowed money to help feed his fellow prophets, but whatever the cause, the fear of the debt collectors was stressing her out. According to the law, an unpaid debt could be paid out by the work of a son: "If one of your countrymen becomes poor among you and sells himself to you, do not make him work as a slave. He is to be treated as a hired worker or a temporary resident among you; he is to work for you until the Year of Jubilee. Then he and his children are to be released, and he will go back to his own clan and to the property of his forefathers" (Lev. 25:39-41).

But unfortunately the law was not exactly being upheld. It was common for the creditor to take back far more than the value of the debt, enslaving as many sons as possible. And as for the Year of Jubilee, well that conveniently never seemed to happen. The widow's worry is understandable, and the miracle provided her with enough oil to sell not only enough to pay the debts but to live on afterward. Her practical need demanded a practical solution. Was this type of work just a sideline for Elisha, something to keep him busy between rebuking sinners and calling down judgment?

> The company of the prophets said to Elisha, "Look, the place where we meet with you is too small for us. Let us go to the Jordan, where each of us can get a pole; and let us build a place there for us to live." And he said, "Go." Then one of them said, "Won't you please come with your servants?" "I will," Elisha replied. And he went with them. They went to the Jordan and began to cut down trees. As one of them was cutting down a tree, the iron axhead fell into the water. "Oh, my lord," he cried out, "it was borrowed!" The man of God asked, "Where did it fall?" When he showed him the place, Elisha cut a stick and threw it there, and made the iron float. "Lift it out," he said. Then the man reached out his hand and took it.
> (2 Kings 6:1-7)

The story moves back to the crew of prophets, who also appear to be rolling their sleeves up for a bit of practical work. Of course, an axhead would have been an expensive tool, and the fact that it was borrowed was another cause of concern as the prospect of slavery came into mind. Elisha had already helped the guys out during a famine by de-poisoning their stew, and the deal here is the same. They are poor and need help, so God helps. It's as simple as that.

There are plenty of other examples of people being used by God to speak on His behalf, delivering words that are sometimes harsh and sometimes full of loving compassion. But we do ourselves a disservice and God an injustice if we believe that all God wants to do is say things to the people in the Church. Elisha is not alone in being used by God to powerfully demonstrate not only the depth of the message that God wants delivered, but the range of people to which He wants it communicated.

The truth of the matter is that we have managed to build up such an elaborate structure that the watering hole mentality has affected almost all of our faith. In telling people that the main aim is to spend time lapping things up at the services, we have provided them with a narrow view of how God's gifts are used. Where God takes the individual and works for the universal, where He takes a gift such as prophecy and uses it to love, heal, judge, forgive, and save, we have turned things on their head. Instead of expressing God's heart through our actions, we have transplanted our hearts onto God's Word. *Stay here*, we say. *Be cozy. Don't leave us.* We push out a message that God's gifts are best used within a church setting.

What's It Like on the Edge?

For every one person who buys in to the idea that church activity is the primary aim of the good Christian, there must be a handful who walk away. There on the edges they are left to feel as if their lack of spiritual zip, zing, and sparkle makes them isolated and unspiritual, and that church (and eventually God) is irrelevant to their lives. Why? Because their life presents them with few outlets for the exercise of their spiritual gifts. I have friends who are fantastic at making others feel relaxed and welcome, ones who love to travel, meet new people, and immerse themselves in new cultures, others who want to see the funny side in everything. And some of these people like to question things, some of them won't accept something as true before they've grappled with it themselves and come up with their own conclusions. Some feel uncomfortable at the thought of letting their emotions out in front of people at meetings, and others feel that they're far less passionate and excited about God than the others at the front. For some the lyrics are hard to sing: the heart-felt devotion, the declaration that God is the number one priority, the sense of victory and unashamed belief in Christ. For some of these people, the first note of the worship will have them chewing over the words and coming up with the conclusion that "I can't sing that."

So what's the solution for these stragglers? Yes, worship is about sacrifice, and yes, there is a case for putting our own selves second in the face of worshiping God, but in leaving these people to struggle on the edges, we do them no favors. We offer them no help to make that step toward finding the songs that they can sing, no ramp up for a step toward expressing the way things are right now before moving on to declaring how they'd like them to be. But the circle continues as many of the people who are attracted to work in the Church as it is today are just the sort of people who like the Church as it is today. So the function remains the same, and the meetings continue to appeal to a select group.

... And in the Middle?

It would be dangerous to assume too much and similarly make our focus too narrow: Some find themselves on the fringes of church life, feeling frustrated and uncomfortable, while others like nothing better than to spend as much time as possible in the thick of it. But most find themselves elsewhere, flitting around, moving in the middle ground between the two. And they share something of the problems of both. There may be a pressure to spend more time at church activities, with the odd absence from home group commented up or the decision not to attend the extra meeting feeling like a personal rejection and failing. For this person there may be the background fear of the ultimate accusation: that they are backsliding. While they might well be doing so, there's also a chance that the absence and backing off from commitments and extra attendance is the sign of an increasingly busy life outside of church. In many places there is support and understanding of this, but in some the mere admission that external influences are dictating church commitments is enough to raise a worried pastoral brow.

I belonged to a church once that made things clear from the start: If you were a member of the church, then you had to take on some role or responsibility. Whether it was setting out the chairs or directing cars around the parking lot, this was the sign that you were a member. And a good idea it was too, helping create a decent team spirit and working against a sense that the congregation were no more than passengers. The trouble came as soon as you wanted to ease off on a particular commitment. Stepping down from the coffee duty became as delicate a negotiation process as securing the release of multiple hostages, with the person asking to leave cast very much as the villain. The mix of membership with activity was a great idea, but perhaps it needed to be applied with just a little less vigor. After all, sometimes life does throw up the unexpected, and sometimes time is precious. We would do well in the Church to remember that it is the Church's function to serve the people who attend as well as the community, not the other way around.

A mid-point stance in relation to the watering hole can add further complications into the mix, as particular needs fail to fit in with the church service. For the person stuck in the midst of non-church culture, it can feel as though issues that need attention are not the sort that belong in church. The ethical and moral considerations of working in such an environment can be pretty rare topics in a sermon, leaving many to struggle to come to terms on their own with life in the gray.

Why Have We Bought into the Watering Hole?

This theory, this idea that the life of both the Christian and the Church involves more than just turning up to meetings is nothing new. It's not exactly groundbreaking, and I doubt it'll have anyone reaching for their highlighting pens. But if that's the case, how come we're still stuck with it? How come we seem to be locked into a cycle of exclusivity and isolation?

My parents' generation found the Church of twenty and thirty years ago a fresh and exciting place. My mom was still living with the wounds of a society that saw couples splitting up with ever increasing ease, and it was with a sense of surprise that she found a church that was loving, warm, open, and very happy for her to express her emotions. How different this place was than the religious institutions she'd been to as a child. They were cold and austere, full of formality and ritual, but in 1974, she discovered something that changed her life forever: Jesus was alive and well in the heart of suburbia. Church became a safe place, a refuge in which she found healing and support. By the time a few years had passed, a new dawn was rising in the form of charismatic renewal. Suddenly there was even greater freedom as the congregation were encouraged to hook up with the Holy Spirit and allow Him time and space to work on their lives. For her and other members of the generation who have divorced more than any other in history, this helped make church a welcome refuge from the pains of the world. And a good thing it was, too.

While I was away with the in-laws recently, we made plans for a church visit on Easter Sunday. They gave us a breakdown of the available options, describing each of the local churches in turn, placing them in one of two categories: "dead" or "alive." I wondered if that was how church felt as the renewal movement swept across the country, with some signing up for this new breath of life while others chose to stay behind with the old ways.

But growing up as I did in a family that went to a fully vibed-up, alive church, my take on things is different than that of my parents'. Church always has been a place of security for me; there never has been an issue about whether or not I could express myself there. I never grew up thinking that church was irrelevant or dull, but the claims of the elder members that it was a safe place and one to be preferred over and above the world inevitably got me thinking.

I left church when I was sixteen and came back when I was nineteen. I didn't come back with my tail between my legs, and I wasn't wounded by the scars of an evil and fallen world. Instead I came back because I found that there was more to life than the highs I'd experienced—both in my time away from church and my pre-rebellion days up in the front during the ministry sessions. You see, I'd grown up convinced that the world was wrong and the Church was right. If I was going to succeed in life, I needed to do my best to remain separate, and that not only included socializing solely with church friends but thinking about a career in the Church and a life spent behind the altar. Eventually the chinks in my armor appeared as those darn heathens failed to live up to the image I'd so carefully constructed. They didn't all worship Satan, and they weren't all murderers. I became friends with them and started to enjoy my time around them. But in my dualistic framework I couldn't have both, and I'd swing from moments of total allegiance to either camp. Eventually my youth leader sat me down and delivered a truly wise and brave word: "The world is spoiling your enjoyment of God, and God is spoiling your enjoyment of the world. Why don't you go? We'll be here when you come back."

I did, and they were. My time away taught me many lessons, some of which I'll bring up later on, but as mentioned before, it wasn't due to a great dose of shame and pain that I returned. I just realized that life without Jesus wasn't as good as life with Him. And this is where the trouble started: I'd done the classic teenage thing and broken away from the parental model, returning ready to do things my own way. But there was still a whiff of "them" vs. "us" hanging around the old place, still a sense that I had some either/or decisions to make about the world outside.

As the years go by and the next generation—who have grown up with a different set of assumptions about the world and the Church—make their mark, the shape of church will change as people begin to get a better perspective on the way things have been going.

N.K. Clifford has this to say: "The evangelical mind has never relished complexity. Indeed its crusading genius, whether in religion or in politics, has always tended toward an over simplification of issues and the substitution of inspiration and zeal for critical analysis and serious reflection."

It's so much easier to live life without facing the difficult questions, and the questions themselves take on different strengths depending on the place in which we choose to answer them. "How do I live a life that pleases God?" is so much easier to answer when the life is lived within the Church. "How does God use me to show His love?" becomes a far harder prospect once the framework of church is removed from the answer. "Does God heal?" "How do I remain pure?" and "How does God speak through me?" all take on a harder edge when asked from the position of a life beyond the meetings. What's more, to truly answer these questions—to live a life that pleases God, to show His love, to be a channel for His healing, to remain pure, and to demonstrate His character—we have to do it to those who need it. At times we'll find them in the Church, but more often than not we simply have to look further afield.

How Should the Watering Hole Look?

"Oh, I don't think we're quite ready for that just yet," said one of my father-in-law's fellow churchgoers after he told them about a new passion for social justice that was gripping the teens and twenties. But if that sort thing is incompatible with the Church, then we've wandered a heck of a long way off course. The Bible gives us a clear picture of how the Church should be functioning, starting with the relationship between the Israelites and their surrounding neighbors. In the same way that they were supposed to act as a shining light for God, giving a strong lead and clear demonstration of the love of God, so too is the modern Church supposed to relate to the rest of the world.

Take praise for example. We're supposed to do it. As "a chosen people, a royal priesthood, a holy nation, a people belonging to God, that you may declare the praises of him who called you out of darkness into his wonderful light" (1 Pet. 2:9). The same goes for establishing the kingdom of God: by sussing out that "the gospel must first be preached to all nations" (Mark 13:10), that "this is what the Lord has commanded us: 'I have made you a light for the Gentiles, that you may bring salvation to the ends of the earth'" (Acts 13:47). It's plain and simple, there in black and white: "Therefore go and make disciples of all nations, baptizing them in the name of the Father and of the Son and of the Holy Spirit" (Matt. 28:19), but if we want it fleshing out a little, a quick glance back at Matthew 25 shows Jesus making it beautifully clear that the kingdom of God bears the marks of unity and sacrifice and care for the poor, oppressed, and unloved.

Our commission, our blueprint for a way of life includes both of these, the praise and the works of the kingdom of God. As the early Church depicted in Acts shows us, when the life of the Church gathered is combined with the life of the Church scattered, the resulting mixture is one seriously tasty cocktail.

What Should the Water Taste Like?

Talking of cocktails, Jesus used the old drink analogy to describe Himself to the woman at the well, saying "but whoever drinks the water I give him will never thirst. Indeed, the water I give him will become in him a spring of water welling up to eternal life" (John 4:14). Of course, she's well up for a bit of thirst-free life, as we all are, and promptly asks Him to furnish her with a couple of pints of His most refreshing draft (or something like that). It's a funny encounter, one retold by John and translated into that slightly whispy language reserved for Jesus. It's as if He is a totally wooden actor, fumbling through a poorly written script: "'I have no husband,' she replied. Jesus said to her, 'You are right when you say you have no husband. The fact is, you have had five husbands, and the man you now have is not your husband. What you have just said is quite true'" (John 4:17-18).

Hardly the most punchy dialogue scene, is it? But we miss the point if we get too hung up on rewrites and Hugh Grant impressions. The fact is that Jesus doesn't avoid the question, He answers it full on: *You want the water of life? You want some, do you? Well, here it is, love: Believe in Me. Worship Me with your whole life. This is key to satisfaction, the tap that turns on the water that never leaves us dissatisfied.* Living for Jesus. Taking His commands to heart. Learning to love Him and show that love to others. Putting selfishness aside and helping others find the water themselves.

The whole Bible provides a narrative around a theme: God's involvement with the world He created. It's not a tale of isolation or separation, not the great divorce, but the faithful love of the ultimate good father for His wayward children. This faithful partner theme is explored superbly in the book of Hosea, and should act as a decent nightcap as the chapter comes to an end.

Hosea was one of the good guys. Living among a bunch of people who were straying from God's path, he faithfully delivered God's Word over many years. Being one of those creative types, God didn't exactly follow standard protocols, and He had our man marry Gomer, a prostitute, to illustrate the tragic demise in the relationship between Israel and God. These were the last days of the Northern Kingdom, and were punctuated by a pretty rank bunch of kings who failed to lead the people back to God.

> Then the Lord said to Hosea, "Call him Jezreel, because I will soon punish the house of Jehu for the massacre at Jezreel, and I will put an end to the kingdom of Israel ... Gomer conceived again and gave birth to a daughter. Then the Lord said to Hosea, "Call her Lo-Ruhamah, for I will no longer show love to the house of Israel, that I should at all forgive them. Yet I will show love to the house of Judah; and I will save them—not by bow, sword or battle, or by horses and horsemen, but by the Lord their God." After she had weaned Lo-Ruhamah, Gomer had another son. Then the Lord said, "Call him Lo-Ammi, for you are not my people, and I am not your God. Yet the Israelites will be like the sand on the seashore, which cannot be measured or counted. In the

place where it was said to them, 'You are not my people,' they will be called 'sons of the living God.'" (Hosea 1:4-10)

Israel's sin was extensive, as is illustrated by the names given to the three children born to Hosea by Gomer. The final line about them not being his people was especially serious as it threatened to break the covenant made with Abraham back in Genesis 22.

Once the children have grown up, Gomer goes back to her old ways, and Hosea's speech is heavy with pain and emotion. Yet within a matter of a few lines, it becomes clear that he is not talking about Gomer, but about the way things look from God's perspective. It appears that Israel has become like a desert, yet when they arrived in the promised land, it was a place of immense fertility. As the Israelites wandered away from God and soaked up other pagan influences, they took part in the Canaanite practice of sacrificing to Baal in return for fertile soil. God had provided something pure, something natural that reflected His great powers as the Creator, and His people threw it back in His face. He offered them a fresh start, a new Eden, and what happened? They brought other gods in. What was fertile and good became corrupt and abused. The Israelites deserved punishment, and God had a few things in mind:

> "Therefore I will take away my grain when it ripens, and my new wine when it is ready. I will take back my wool and my linen, intended to cover her nakedness. So now I will expose her lewdness before the eyes of her lovers; no one will take her out of my hands. I will stop all her celebrations: her yearly festivals, her New Moons, her Sabbath days—all her appointed feasts. I will ruin her vines and her fig trees, which she said were her pay from her lovers; I will make them a thicket, and wild

animals will devour them. I will punish her for the days she burned incense to the Baals; she decked herself with rings and jewelry, and went after her lovers, but me she forgot," declares the Lord. (Hosea 2:9-13)

But then something remarkable follows: "'Therefore I am now going to allure her; I will lead her into the desert and speak tenderly to her ... In that day,' declares the Lord, 'you will call me "my husband"; you will no longer call me "my master"'" (Hosea 2:14,16).

What an odd word to kick off with: *therefore*. Shouldn't it be more like, "You deserve all this punishment, *but instead* I am going to have you back?" Shouldn't He be having them back in spite of what they deserve? The truth is a little less black and white, with the answer being found in the Hebrew word often used to describe God's love: *hesed*. When we talk about love, the word on its own fails to do justice to that which is at the heart of God. Take a look at Jesus on the cross, crucified "because God so loved the world." The original Hebrew sheds light on the different textures of love; there's *ahba*, which means affection for people and things, including sexual attraction. There's *rahamin*, which points to a sense of pity for someone helpless, as a parent loves a child. And then there's something else altogether: *hesed*, a type of love that involves choosing, that takes the strength, courage, and determination to fulfill a relationship contract. When Hosea married Gomer, it was from *ahba* and *rahamin* love. After this passage God tells him to bring her back, *hesed* love in full effect.

But there's no chance of being left in the dark. Through Hosea God explains precisely where they went wrong in the past:

Hear the word of the Lord, you Israelites, because the Lord has a charge to bring against you who live in the land: "There is no faithfulness, no love, no acknowledgment of God in the land. There is only cursing, lying and murder, stealing and adultery; they break all bounds, and bloodshed follows bloodshed. Because of this the land mourns, and all who live in it waste away; the beasts of the field and the birds of the air and the fish of the sea are dying. But let no man bring a charge, let no man accuse another, for your people are like those who bring charges against a priest." (Hosea 4:1-4)

A lack of "faithfulness ... love ... acknowledgment of God," which some take to mean that the Israelites lacked honesty, *hesed* love, and any knowledge of God. This had caused them to wander away from God and straight into His judgment. The lethal cocktail left them a barely recognizable reflection of the people they were supposed to be.

If the Church is the new Israel, is there any chance that we could be due a similar summing up? Could a lack of honesty, self-sacrificing love, and knowledge of God be something that rings a bell? Are we sure that we're brimming with an openness and honesty about not only the struggles that we all face but the challenge that God has given us? Is our love the sort that searches out the prodigals, that finds the people who deserve judgment, and therefore welcomes them back? Do we know God, do we act on the truth that we find in the Bible, the imperative to follow the lead of His Son Jesus? Could the fact that we're found wanting when it comes to these be a sign that it's time to move church away from the watering hole?

"We need to refine the way we live and the way we act in the face of the normal world."

3

How Do I Look at Others?

The Mask of Evangelism

Looking back on it now, it's a wonder that I ever managed to survive at school. My early teenage years were marked by so fierce a brand of spiritual earnestness that I lived for the weekends. While classmates would come in on Monday morning and tell of another sixty-five hours spent watching television, thinking about how to talk to girls, and trying to catch a glimpse of their middle-aged neighbor through the bathroom window, I'd be chewing over an action-packed, five-star treat of a weekend. Friday night meant church youth group; Saturday meant church friends; Saturday night meant more church friends; and Sunday meant double church with extra church friends after the service. These were the days that kept me going, the times when I felt I could be myself. In the early years, school was just an inconvenience, something that got in the way of the important stuff in life.

But the real reason I question how I survived is my masks. They were vicious, scary, unfeeling, and more than often just plain weird. Let me explain: It was all about evangelists. You see, our church often had visiting evangelists come along and deliver a pep talk, offer a few pointers, and sum up a five-point plan for local revival that anyone could master. They were often tanned, frequently good looking, and always topped up with a level of self-assurance that made them simply irresistible. There was no doubt in my mind at all: I wanted to be like them, and that was final. While other kids were putting up posters of Kevin Keegan, "Bubbly" Samantha Fox, and cute little teddy bears saying "I Wuv You" to each other, I was showing my allegiance to the heroes of my life in slightly less subtle ways. Door-knocking at dusk, casting out demons in the restrooms, and slipping tracts into lockers when no one was looking. I was a one-man tsunami of revival, and if anyone got in my way, I'd flatten them with some devastatingly spiritual quip plucked straight from the mouth of whichever evangelist was top of my league at that particular moment.

It didn't work for me like it did for them. When told by the tanned evo-hero, somehow what started out as a request for directions always ended up with sobbing, repenting, and salvation right there, right then. With me, using the same lines, the same half-smile, the same desperate desire for people to come to know God, what started as directions ended up as something worse.

"Hey, Borlase. Where's our math class meeting?"

"I can see into your soul, Darren."

"What?"

"The pain inside is God's doorbell. Won't you let him in, Darren?"

*

It never worked, and no matter how hard I tried, putting on the old evangelism mask always seemed to leave me looking at best deranged and at worst in line for a kicking. And when being considered deranged is your best-case scenario, you know that things aren't going too well.

But in some way, these incidents of clicking on the old mask and adopting a different persona in the hope that it would reap the souls have stayed with me ever since. Even more embarrassing is the fact that at times it feels as though I haven't moved on from those unnatural, uncomfortable days at all. I still feel the pressure to tell others about God, but so often it fails to feel natural, as if I need to stop what I'm doing and self-consciously adopt a whole new me. It's frustrating to say the least, especially when I still get that look that says "somebody save me from this deranged man" coming straight back at me.

Somewhere deep down there's another voice, one that suggests that things don't have to be this way. Can I be a good Christian without reading from a three-minute conversion script? Can I be honest with people, telling them about my struggles as well as about the things that are going well? Can I be a good Christian without having to use the evangelism mask; is there any way that it can be a little more *me* and less *mask*?

Further Tales of Failed Masks

Want to know the truth? I've never clinched the deal with a friend, never told him the spiritual score and led him to the Lord. Actually that's not entirely true, as there was one friend way back who was interested in coming along to church. I deliberated, taking ages to get back to him. How come? I was scared. Church life was so nice; I had my friends just right and enjoyed things exactly the way they were; why did I want someone coming in from the outside and messing it all up? Would I have to bring him along every week, babysitting for the rest of my life? What about my church friends ... would they like him, was he cool enough? Some people talk about hiding their church lives from their nine-to-five lives. For me it was the other way around, almost not wanting to let that part of me in. But eventually this friend came along, stood up when the call came, and said the prayer. I stopped hanging out with him soon after and barely saw him once we changed grade levels. I wish the story didn't end like that, but it does. Want to know the hardest thing? I liked him. He was a good friend. I failed him.

My first evo-hero was Luis Palo, the South American evangelist. I went along to a meeting he was speaking at when I was about eight years old. The venue was QPR football stadium in London, and I can clearly remember associating the crowds and terraces with football violence and rival teams. I was scared that at any minute the Methodist crew was going to start hurling chairs, bottles, and sharpened Bibles at the Baptists, while we Anglicans got caught in the crossfire. It was a scary time, and when Luis told all who weren't saved to come down onto the pitch and stand in front of the stage, there was no way I was going to disobey. I'd been a Christian for about five years already and had said the prayer on numerous occasions, so I knew the drill. I can still remember the faint droop of disappointment that crept over the face of the woman praying with me as I told her that I already was a Christian but was doing it "just to be sure."

Somehow I got a taste for it, despite the fear and sense of imminent personal danger, and vowed to become Carlos Blasé, the next big thing on the evangelists' circuit. Of course, everyone knows that a good evangelist needs a gimmick, whether it's singing, being argumentative or just plain smarmy, and I planned on adopting my own affectation. The way I saw it, I was going to be the first evangelist under ten years old who harnessed the full potential of the communications revolution. I was going to fuse prophetic insight with pure reliance on the Spirit of God in such a way that I would be known as the Combine Harvester of Souls. Or so I thought. In reality I just put on some worship music, flicked through the phone book, picked a number at random, and held the receiver to my stereo, allowing the Lord to do the rest. Funnily enough, the thrill wore off after a few sessions.

Then there was the time I misunderstood what some guy said during a midweek meeting. He was banging on about evangelism, saying how hard he found it and all that, when he mentioned a fact that made me sit up and pay attention: two-thirds of people become Christians through relationships. Something for us all to think about, he suggested, and we moved into a time of quiet reflection where we could ponder how such a revelation could impact our lives. I was off running with my new idea: If relationships were the fertile compost out of which a harvest might grow, then who was I to ignore the facts? I scanned through all the potential girlfriends I knew at college and decided to aim my spiritual shark fin in the direction of the most hedonistic one of them all. As the time of quiet reflection drew to a close and people were invited to share their thoughts about their future activities, I jumped in first and delivered a long and detailed account of my seduction technique, leaving out none of the details, ending with a hope that she would have a few friends with whom I could also get jiggy for the Lord. Finding out in front of all those people that this was a slightly narrower definition of relationships than he had intended was not a pleasant experience.

Later as I left college, I moved back home and hooked up with some friends who were starting a new church. They were fired up about something they were calling friendship evangelism and were running a café event with the aim of meeting new people and providing a platform from which to invite them along to a church service. It was a simple plan: set up a venue in a local sports club or hotel, serve a little food and drink, get a band together to play a few chart tunes, and let the rest of the team chat and get to know people. It worked well and pulled in plenty of fourteen- and fifteen-year-olds, many of whom had heard about the café through the school.

I struggled. I was a twenty-two-year-old fresh out of college. I'd studied English, drove a brown Metro, and fancied myself as a bit of a Renaissance man: writer of poetry (bad), lover of funk (rare), and creator of fine food (French). In short, I was a bit of a prat, but in general it was an improvement from my cardigan and tweed phase, so there was relatively little to complain about. Given my tastes, therefore, it was hardly surprising that I struggled to really connect with the fourteen- and fifteen-year-old scallies who attended the café. I developed a sophisticated range of techniques that helped me avoid the situation of actually having to talk one-on-one with the little darlings, and I would spend the whole evening in a state that combined the pain of long-term constipation with the unease of extreme diarrhea. I would tune my guitar obsessively. I would make a trip to the bathroom last fifteen minutes. I would latch on to any of my fellow churchgoers who would let me act as wing man. Actually wing man's a little too impressive a title, as in truth I was more like the awkward foreign exchange student who hangs on like a leech, unable to communicate on a level other than by grinning inanely and mumbling something about how he likes Liverpool FC. I was a complete waste of space and liked nothing less than the Friday night ritual of friendship evangelism.

But there was more to my frustration than a simple age gap. I'd left university the year before, and many of my friends were still there, completing their final year after spending a year in France as part of their course. University was close too, just a thirty-minute drive away, and Friday night was always the big night down there. Unfortunately, my involvement at the café project ruled me out of those nights back at college as there seemed to be a strong link between commitment to the project, commitment to the church, and commitment to God. And so I settled down with a double dose of guilt: that which came from feeling as though I was not "on message"—that because I was not happy there, my faith was somehow inferior—and that which was the result of seeing my friendships from university days slip away. If the Church was supposed to be so committed to friendship evangelism, I thought, why were my real friendships dying a slow death from lack of attention?

Inevitably the guilt turned to bitterness, and by the time I worked out why I felt the way I did, I was walking around the café with a face like a slapped bum giving off "I hate this" vibes by the bucket load. If only I'd been able to understand things a little earlier, I am sure that the situation would have been different and that the church would have understood, but as it was, I simply got stuck into thinking that friendship evangelism was a complete waste of time.

Do I Really Have to Evangelize?

At my worst, the pulse raging with the frustrations of a life out of control, I wondered long and hard about the point of evangelism. Surprisingly, I completely missed it. To me it was nothing more than a shallow show of false emotion, of friendship with strings or platform-performance that only cared about the numbers coming up not the people going back. All I wanted to do was be myself, hang out with my friends, be a true and genuine friend without any of the heavy stuff that the church seemed so keen on loading us up with. But I never was much good at putting myself in other people's positions, and it has taken years for the frustrations to filter down into anything more sensible.

Evangelism might be one of those terms that we find exceedingly unhelpful, but it's clearly printed on the menu. Correction, it's firmly stamped on our frames. Evangelism is not an optional extra, something that we can pick and choose, leaving aside if we don't quite feel up for it at any one time. And Paul's line about the calling of "some to be evangelists, some to be prophets ..." in Ephesians 4 doesn't let us off the hook either, no matter how hard I wished it did all those years ago. No, evangelism—telling, showing, and inspiring people about God, acting as His signposts—is something we Christians have to do. But before this becomes the sort of chapter I would previously have burned, it's worth mentioning a few "yes, but ..."s in response to the million-dollar question: Do I really have to evangelize?

Yes, but ... what's the motive? Strikes me that if all we ever do is see evangelism as a chore, if we separate it from the essential truth that it is about relationship—both with God and others—then it's always going to be a bit rough. Are we doing it so that we can simply get it done? Is it something to be checked off and forgotten about for the next week/month/year? If this is the mindset out of which we operate, it's bound to be hard work.

Yes, but ... who is doing it? Have we become so hooked into this idea of using a mask, of adopting a persona that doesn't fit? Relying on a model that is fake and transparent leads us down an unpleasant avenue, one which (as we'll see later) is at odds with the way Jesus behaved. Sure, He was honest about the need for lifestyle change in people, but the Gospels never give us reason to believe that He switched into "the mode" or that He made an effort to put on His cheesiest grin for the sake of the punters.

Yes, but ... just what does it mean to evangelize? If Paul makes that distinction in Ephesians about the importance of unity through diversity, singling some people out as evangelists, does that really mean it can only be done in one way? It seems to me that he was referring more to the bold proclaimers there, the ones with a God-given gift for presenting the Gospel in a clear, logical, and lucid form. It's true that some of us are called to be the up-front bods, the communicators who deliver, expand, or inspire the message. But they are part of the team, just as much as those for whom the idea of doing likewise would have them quaking in their boots. You see, if we reckon that evangelism is only about telling people about Jesus, explaining about the cross, sin, forgiveness, salvation, and all that, then we're stuffed. After all, is Christianity only about saying a prayer? Does it stop once you've signed up? Of course not, and the Bible is full of top-notch examples of people demonstrating the love of God in a multitude of practical, imaginative, and caring ways. God, the creator of the world, is often just one or two steps ahead of us when it comes to carrying out His work in a variety of ways. Which is quite frustrating really as it makes it increasingly difficult to pin Him down and say how He does or does not move.

Yes, but ... the aim is not to be so well disguised that no one can tell the difference between us and the rest of the population. I suppose that the opposite of masked-up evangelism is relational stuff, the type where character and integrity shout loudest, but there's always the danger that things can go a little too far. For the well-camouflaged Christian, the killer blow goes something along the lines of "I really like your faith 'cuz it just doesn't seem like a big deal ..." It's tough to bounce back, but vital that the warning gets heeded. The aim is not to blend, not even to be accepted, but to be authentic.

Ditch the Mask?

There's plenty of good stuff to be found at the heart of the proclamation model. All that hardcore evangelizing, the standing up in front of the masses, giving them analogies and information that can help bring the issue to the front of the mind is totally valid. This is a faith worth dying for, let alone losing a little street cred, and the boldness and willingness to speak out is a lesson that applies to all Christians in all situations. But there is a danger that lurks in the shadows, one which threatens the strength of the work itself.

Allow me to digress. When I was on the verge of coming back to Christianity, I was at a conference. I had turned up due to the persistent nagging of a couple of good friends and spent the week wandering around the outside of meetings. As time moved on and I felt more comfortable, I moved further inside the buildings where the meetings were being held, keen to observe what was going on and wonder how I felt about it all. It was midway through the week that I was doing just this, staring about, when a man came up and told me that the Lord had told him to come and pray for me. He had bad breath, and I was really doing fine on my own, just soaking it all in and gradually getting used to the idea of being back in church after three years out of it. I mumbled something about not needing any prayer, but he was insistent.

I gave in, and he launched off. We had it all: prayers of rebuke, prayers of repentance, prayers of prophecy, prayers of warfare, prayers of inspiration for more prayers. He was carpet-bombing me with prayers, surely in the hope that at least something was right. After a few minutes and a particularly long ranting prayer about the need to be careful if I ever met a man named Gavin with a yellow rucksack, I opened my eyes to see whether he might need some medical attention. He had his eyes open too, but instead of being cast in my general direction they were scanning the arena presumably for something more interesting than me. I sat and watched, and he kept on praying. I tried coughing gently, but he kept on praying and watching the sound engineer at work a few yards in front. Eventually I slipped off to the side and left him to it. He may still be there to this day.

OK, so it has nothing to do with evangelism, but it has everything to do with masks. When we forget about the people and concentrate more on the delivery, when we adopt the persona instead of recognizing the individual, we set ourselves on a course that runs straight away from a biblical model. Of course, this makes things considerably harder work: If the aim is simply getting random strangers to say a prayer, then there is little need to be nice. If all we have to do in order to check off our evangelistic duties for a month is take a carload along to the next stadium gig, then we successfully manage to absolve ourselves of all responsibility when it comes to living an authentic life. Invitations are so much easier than integrity.

For many people, while the model of platform evangelism still has a place, the realization has taken root inside of them that this is but one part of the pie. Singing "let the streets resound with singing" has shown a desire to take things, not just to bring the punters in. After all, how does the idea of clicking into evangelism mode work with a Gospel that preaches inclusion and "go" rather than seclusion and lack of compassion? Jesus placed maximum importance on the fact that Christianity was for all, and He worked hard to make it an accessible message for outcasts, the oppressed, and the despised. Just look at the way He addresses Zaccheus' insecurity head on, signaling him out from the crowd, choosing to spend time with him in his home, surrounded by the fruits of his misguided energies. It is precisely this type of model of concern, understanding, and relationship that is leading many away from the concept of evangelism as a program or part to play and into something that manages to integrate a readiness to spread the Gospel with a desire to do it as naturally as possible. Should we ditch the mask? Absolutely. Why don't we try going with our instincts a little more, harnessing the fuel of the Gospel that says Jesus died for all of us?

Proclamation and friendship evangelism programs have their place. We should not give them up or throw them to the dogs, but in taking off the mask we realize that evangelism is something that should be able to sit comfortably in every aspect of our lives. Whether it's at school, college, or work, socializing with friends or colleagues, we need to refine the way we live and the way we act in the face of the normal world. What's more, while the proclamation and friendship programs should continue, we would do well to adopt the strengths of each in order to reinforce a way of living that works in the real world. From the proclamation crew, let's take the boldness and reliance on the Holy Spirit for inspiration; from the friendship evangelism model, let's take the passion to get outside of our cozy cliques and sacrifice our time and energy for others. That would be a start, wouldn't it?

Life Without the Mask

If we are going to lose the masks, if we are going to learn how to present ourselves in a far more authentic way—whether that's for more formal methods of friendship or proclamation or just being friends with someone long term—then we need to come to grips with some fundamental issues.

Who Am I Called To?

There's an exercise used by family therapists and others that might be worth thinking about. On a piece of paper draw yourself in the center—not a full self-portrait, just something to represent you. Next, think over all the people who are part of your life, and draw them on the paper, placing them as close to or as far away from your name as you think reflects the real-life situation. Once that's done, draw a line between yourself and each person named on the paper, with the line helping to describe the relationship. If you think it's a particularly difficult relationship, you might like to draw a jagged line between your two names, while if it's a good one you might just opt for a straight line. If you feel as though the relationship is a one-way affair— with one party putting more in than the other gives back—try putting in arrows along the line. Use your imagination as much as you like to flesh things out.

We worry a lot about who we are called to. With the masks on and the timer running, there can be an immense pressure to choose the right person who will yield a decent result in a short period of time. But common sense suggests that the people we stand a far better chance of relating to are right under our noses. The presence of common ground—whether that's an interest, shared history, personality, or circumstance—is as good a place as any to start.

But for a while, the Church has resisted this type of logic to some extent. Evangelism church-style happens on our turf, on our terms. And, of course, it's far safer this way. The guy who leads my church has gotten in trouble more often than he'd care to remember over suggesting that the Church needs to take a hint from the life of Jesus and spend more time out with the godless than we currently do. Hoards of scared parents and worried youth workers queue up to remind him of the dangers that lie out in the big bad world, and in many cases they are right. But look back at the friendship map—presuming you've done it—who do you see? Any people with whom you've got a relationship already, but who could do with getting to know Jesus? With this in mind, going out and doing the stuff away from the church-run program moves things away from this idea of "church good, world bad."

How Harsh Can I Be?

Our attitude toward others is central to presenting an honest face, and it's the topic we focus on in the next chapter, but it's worth flagging up one idea in advance. Part of pursuing genuine friendship involves an element of unconditionality, but just how compatible is this with much of our understanding of how things should be done? Does our friendship really come with strings attached? Is there really a "save by" date on every Christian/non-Christian relationship?

Some may argue that a rejection of God should be taken seriously, that a person who rejects the message should be shaken off like dust from the sandals as the good Christian moves off to find better pasture. But how does this compare with that ultimate of on/off relationships: God and Israel? If ever there was a case for God kicking Israel into next week, it's throughout the Bible. *Ah*, you might say, *surely God did reject them by sending Jesus*. As much as that might appeal to our supremacist Western mindset, it's not actually true. Yes, God did eventually bypass the Israelites, but only in as much that the task they were due to complete—acting as a shining light of salvation to all other nations—was taken away from being their job alone and opened up to the Church at large, including both Jew and non-Jew alike.

The book of Amos has something further to add to the debate. After a preliminary warm-up during which the prophet conveys God's anger with the injustice of Israel's neighbors, the book shifts focus away from the foreigners and onto the cheering Israelites, enjoying the news of their hated enemies getting a divine telling off. True enough, the Israelites enjoyed a privileged position in God's eyes, and He had done much to help them.

> "I destroyed the Amorite before them, though he was tall as the cedars and strong as the oaks. I destroyed his fruit above and his roots below. I brought you up out of Egypt, and I led you for forty years in the desert to give you the land of the Amorites. I also raised up prophets from among your sons and Nazirites from among your young men. Is this not true, people of Israel?" declares the Lord. (Amos 2:9-11)

But their position, while it may have been special, did not offer them a get-out-of-jail-free card when it came to either their sin or God's judgment:

> This is what the Lord says: "For three sins of Israel, even for four, I will not turn back my wrath. They sell the righteous for silver, and the needy for a pair of sandals. They trample on the heads of the poor as upon the dust of the ground and deny justice to the oppressed. Father and son

use the same girl and so profane my holy name. They lie down beside every altar on garments taken in pledge. In the house of their god they drink wine taken as fines."
(Amos 2:6-8)

These sins—slavery, greed, oppression, sexual immorality, using ill-gotten gains in places that were supposed to be holy, and failing to take things on trust—are all bound up with selfishness. The Israelites had become so self-referring, so sensitized to their own desires and ambitions, that as individuals they had failed to take account of the inherent individuality of others. Instead of people, they saw a way of getting rich; instead of God, they saw a means of satisfying their own senses. And what does God have to say about this? "This is what the Lord says: 'As a shepherd saves from the lion's mouth only two leg bones or a piece of an ear, so will the Israelites be saved, those who sit in Samaria on the edge of their beds and in Damascus on their couches'" (Amos 3:12).

Oh, that's not too bad then, eh? At least there's a bit of bone left. Not quite; if a shepherd brought back a few sheep bones after an attack from a wild animal, he was covering himself. The bones were proof that the sheep had been entirely destroyed, that there was nothing left, and that it hadn't simply wandered off. Doesn't look so good for Israel, does it?

The smug attitude that the enemies were wrong and that the Jews were right brought them into direct conflict with God's judgment. Sin against people is sin against God, and the idea that they were due special treatment got comprehensively blown out of the water. But what's this got to do with us? According to Amos, on the surface the Israelites weren't up to their eyes in sin and debauchery: in fact, they were actually quite good at putting on a good show. They did the feasts, the offerings, the songs, and all that religious jazz, but it was not enough to fool God:

> I hate, I despise your religious feasts; I cannot stand your assemblies. Even though you bring me burnt offerings and grain offerings, I will not accept them. Though you bring choice fellowship offerings, I will have no regard for them. Away with the noise of your songs! I will not listen to the music of your harps. But let justice roll on like a river, righteousness like a never-failing stream! Did you bring me sacrifices and offerings forty years in the desert, O house of Israel? (Amos 5:21-24)

Life behind the mask—hiding behind the ritual or the action—is not enough to fool God. He sees behind and demands so much more of His people. If we are to take the call of Jesus to "go and make disciples of all nations" (Matt. 28:19) seriously, then we'd better make sure that we are doing a lot more than relying on our talent for putting on slick presentations and programs. We'd better make sure the lifestyle matches up.

How Did Jesus Do It?

The Bible can seem fairly barren when searching for examples of friendship that speak to us today. Culture specific to young people as we know it simply didn't exist, and life appears to be far more focused on work than leisure. So what are we to take from it when on the hunt for tips and treats that will help us live life full of authenticity?

"Once when Jesus was praying in private and his disciples were with him, he asked them, 'Who do the crowds say I am?' They replied, 'Some say John the Baptist; others say Elijah; and still others, that one of the prophets of long ago has come back to life.'

'But what about you?' he asked. 'Who do you say I am?' Peter answered, 'The Christ of God'" (Luke 9:18-20).

This story also gets covered in Matthew 16 and Mark 8. It's a key point in the evolution of Jesus' mission. It marks the transition from performing the prophetic acts to fulfilling His role as the Messiah, and comes just after the disciples have been sent out on their first ministry trip.

If you asked this "Who do you say Jesus is?" question today, you'd come back with an armful of varied answers. Bearded nut ... good man ... prophet ... Santa Claus' PR man ... macrobiotic vegan in sandals. But back then, with Peter in the hot seat, the answer to the first question is similar to these: confused, misinformed, and inaccurate. When the focus turns from second-guessing the chat on the street to answering for himself, Peter comes up trumps. Matthew has him saying "you are the Christ, the Son of the living God" (16:16) and Mark goes for "you are the Christ" (8:29). The point? The answer was based on evidence. Peter had spent plenty of time in Jesus' company. He—along with the other disciples— had seen Jesus in action, healing, feeding, caring. It was the close-up view that made the answer both personal and correct. In short, Jesus showed who He was by the way He lived His life.

Forgive me for being a little selective here, bending the Bible to suit my goal, but it seems that we can take three simple episodes in Jesus' life that help illustrate the point. First is that passage in John 2 where Jesus visits the wedding at Cana. The story's well known and has added beef to many a wedding sermon.

> On the third day a wedding took place at Cana in Galilee. Jesus' mother was there, and Jesus and his disciples

had also been invited to the wedding. When the wine was gone, Jesus' mother said to him, "They have no more wine." "Dear woman, why do you involve me?" Jesus replied. "My time has not yet come." His mother said to the servants, "Do whatever he tells you." Nearby stood six stone water jars, the kind used by the Jews for ceremonial washing, each holding from twenty to thirty gallons. Jesus said to the servants, "Fill the jars with water"; so they filled them to the brim. Then he told them, "Now draw some out and take it to the master of the banquet." They did so, and the master of the banquet tasted the water that had been turned into wine. He did not realize where it had come from, though the servants who had drawn the water knew. Then he called the bridegroom aside and said, "Everyone brings out the choice wine first and then the cheaper wine after the guests have had too much to drink; but you have saved the best till now." This, the first of his miraculous signs, Jesus performed in Cana of Galilee. He thus revealed his glory, and his disciples put their faith in him. (John 2:1-11)

The key point? Jesus had compassion. To run out of wine at a wedding banquet was a social faux pas of almost criminal proportions, one that the father of the bride would have found mighty difficult to live down. What's more, Jesus chose the servants as the miracle couriers, with them and them alone knowing what had happened. To everyone else, it was a mere oddity that the best should be saved till last, but to the servants this was a powerful message: the instruments that were previously central to religious ceremony were no longer needed. Jesus was in town to reframe the way people viewed everything, from who would be used by God to how people could be cleansed. Weddings are often marked by a touch of chaos, and it seems that this was no different, yet the breadth of God's message was fully comfortable right at the heart of it.

> As Jesus was on his way, the crowds almost crushed him. And a woman was there who had been subject to bleeding for twelve years, but no one could heal her. She came up behind him and touched the edge of his cloak, and immediately her bleeding stopped. "Who touched me?" Jesus asked. When they all denied it, Peter said, "Master, the people are crowding and pressing against you." But Jesus said, "Someone touched me; I know that power has gone out from me." Then the woman, seeing that she could not go unnoticed, came trembling and fell at his feet. In the presence of all the people, she told why she had touched him and how she had been instantly healed. Then he said to her, "Daughter, your faith has healed you. Go in peace." (Luke 8:42-48)

Again, we see Jesus do something different. The woman was ritually unclean and therefore on the margins of society, living with the burden of both poverty and humiliation. To notice someone touching Him in the crowd was remarkable, but his language pushes our point even further. "Who touched me?" He asked, as it was the real Him that she touched. The woman knew who He was, knew that He had the power to heal, and it was those characteristics that defined the man she was touching.

> One of the criminals who hung there hurled insults at him: "Aren't you the Christ? Save yourself and us!" But the other criminal rebuked him. "Don't you fear God," he said, "since you are under the same sentence? We

are punished justly, for we are getting what our deeds deserve. But this man has done nothing wrong." Then he said, "Jesus, remember me when you come into your kingdom." Jesus answered him, "I tell you the truth, today you will be with me in paradise." (Luke 23:39-43)

"When Jesus saw his mother there, and the disciple whom he loved standing nearby, he said to his mother, 'Dear woman, here is your son,' and to the disciple, 'Here is your mother.' From that time on, this disciple took her into his home" (John 19:26-27).

Finally we come to the account of Jesus on the cross. In the midst of excruciating agony, we see a man who is capable of thinking of others. As well as the thought for His mother's future security, Jesus shows compassion to the criminal. It's astounding that He could do this, but it once again rams home the message that Jesus was the most selfless human who ever lived.

So what are we saying? Do we have to recreate the miracles of Jesus at every available opportunity? Should we adopt the technique of posing the old "Who do people say I am?" question whenever the conversation begins to dry up? Should we opt for the beard and sandals look in the hope of winning more souls for the kingdom? Do we have to be Jesus? Thankfully not—that's His job, and ours is to follow the lead, not head it all up ourselves. Instead, we can take more readily applicable lessons from the model of Jesus' life that helped confirm to Peter exactly who He said He was. When in the middle of the crazy scene like the wedding, with the laughs and frivolity, when it's someone else's responsibility to sort out the arrangements, and we're just there to kick back and take things easy, do we remember who we are? Are people having a better time because we are there? Are we jostling for position at the top table or happily there with those lower down the chain? Are we aware of the breadth of God's message, ready and able to show His love and compassion in all manner of unusual ways?

Or take the crowd scenario. When everything is going well for us, when it seems like everyone rates us and wants to give a little pat on the back, are we inflating our own ego or looking out for the loveless? Are we full of ourselves or ready to give out at a moment's notice? Are we listening to those telling us how great we are or aware of how desperate the need is around us?

Or pain. When life feels as though it simply cannot get any worse, are we wallowing in self-pity or looking out for others? Are we looking down in dejection or keeping an eye out for who God might want to speak to? Are we focusing on the pain of the present or thinking of the master plan of heaven?

If evangelism is simply showing Jesus to a world in need, then there are some pretty clear guides for us to follow here: compassion, selflessness, integrity. Do we want to live life without the mask of performance, affectation, or pretense? Then perhaps we all need to get down to the business of showing what the true Christian should look like.

"God's heart beats for all."

4

How Do Others Actually See Me?

The Truth About Respect

At different times and in different ways I've been guilty of missing the God-made mark by a spectacular margin. I've taken various crumbs of theology and constructed my own bite-sized model of God, me, and the universe. Swinging from one extreme to another, there have been times when I've been so convicted of my sin, so aware of just how far away I am from godly perfection that I've had little choice but to consider myself a worm. So that's been nice. But at other times I've been further away from the position than seems humanly possible: *I am God's child*, I've told myself. And that makes me very, very special. More special than the rest of you miserable lot ... Sorry about that. OK, so it might be a tad extreme, but spiritual arrogance really is a much nicer thought with which to whittle away an afternoon than all that self-deprecation stuff. But the trouble is that my life has not been spent in an isolation tank. People have seen me up close and have caught both the fire of my self-loathing and the freeze of my superiority. Here's an example:

I am a fatherless child.
I am proud.

I am so far away from being whole.
My mouth speaks in lies.
Lust fills my eyes.
I am so far away from being whole.
I say I'm your servant,
Delight in being your child.
But again and again I serve myself.
And so I will burn
In the fire of your return
As again and again I save myself.
[October 1992]

I know it's asking a lot, but if you could look just beyond the absolute horror of the poetry for a moment, you'll see a young man not exactly sure of his position in the grand scheme of things. I read it out loud to a friend of mine I was living with at the time, and even by his standards—brought up in a Jesuit school and repeatedly reminded that he was but a maggot on God's great honey-glazed ham of life—it was, as he said, "a bit much." A bit much? Thankfully I was prevented from showing him any of my other work (like the epic ballad "The Year of One Thousand Plagues") as he was too busy rereading the "poem" and laughing hysterically. My pride was wounded, and I went back upstairs to carry on feeling bad about myself in private.

But it wasn't always like that. There were times when I would have been far more likely to have written about his own soul rather than my own, and the verdict would have been even more damning. After all, if that's what he thought about me, he should try hearing what God thought about him. A sinful Catholic with no church attendance ... let me see, that would make him the proud owner of a one-way ticket to hell! Years previously I used to wander around the playground during school lunch break, avoiding the sting of football-in-face and wondering about just how many of my fellow school attendees would be standing with me on the last day (and I wasn't talking about the end of summer term, either). I concluded that out of the one thousand guys there, I was the only one who really knew the score. Sure, some of them may have been Christians and were churchgoers, but when it came down to it, it was only myself and the psychotic physics teacher Mr. Gable who were the true believers on the premises. Gable and I were the only ones on the true path to eternal life. I got the shock of my life when I first saw *The Matrix* years later: all those scenes of people going about their business unaware of the truth that existed just beyond them summed up precisely how I felt as a small boy. While I never got so far as developing a full-on messiah complex, at times I was certainly well on the way to the belief that all others were little more than a virus on this sin-encrusted world.

Wising up to the fact that we may actually not be quite the naked Christians that we want to be is an unpleasant thought. With our off-center views about what we think God's idea of success is and our tendency to present people with a pre-made mask that hides our true personality, these contorted backroom workings are bound to leak out. Much as we might like to think that others see us as cool, calm, assured, and simply marvelous, quite often they see something completely different. How do others actually see us? In my own life, I know that the twin extremes of arrogance and a lack of self-worth have underwritten my faith in God. When others have looked, they have seen right through my disguises and ambitions to a central truth that should really have no place within the faith: a lack of respect.

Lack of respect? Christians? Sounds like an odd mix to some, and in all my time at church I don't think I can recall having heard much said about it. But this is the core that infects the surrounding flesh. If we hope to be able to strip down and show others who we really are, we all need to ask some hard questions. Is arrogance ever at home within us? Do we at times lack the benefit of a more accurate view of how God sees us? Do these problems affect the way we view others? Does this mean we close down shop and declare that God is in everyone and everything? How did Jesus find the balance between love and judgment?

The Effects of Ego-Overdrive

It's not uncommon to find ourselves feeling as though we have more in common with the Old Testament Israelites than the New Testament heroes. Sure a few of those New Testament chaps got martyred—earning some serious religious conflict points—but it was the Old Testament ones who really knew how to put on a good fight. Theirs seems to be so much more the language of war and annihilation, of sieges, enemies, and destruction.

We like to pick up this idea of the fight and run with it ourselves, but instead of Babylonians, Syrians, and Egyptians we pick on an enemy far closer to home. The number one evil for many of us is that big, bad world outside. For argument's sake, we'll call it contemporary culture, and we see it wherever we look: clubs, media, attitudes of the people. We'll look at these attitudes in depth later on, but in short we can be tempted to adopt a black-and-white approach to things. Whether it's our worried eyes scanning the TV listings for programs that might not be too bad on our souls or a desire to retreat into a sanctified and sanitized version of the world at large, we sign up to the old chestnut called Dualism. Life is black and white; spirit is better than flesh; God only ever deals in spirit; and the devil works through flesh. Mixed with the ever-fruity Gnosticism, it plagued the early Church and was a reason for so much New Testament teaching on issues of personal holiness, responsibility, and the fact that salvation is not something that is earned.

If it all sounds like too much of an outdated-ism to be in full effect today, then all we need to do is look at the Christian music scene. There we can find "Christian" versions of all types of mainstream artists. Delirious? is the Christian Radiohead, World Wide Message Tribe does a Christian Prodigy while dc Talk and others play Christian versions of U.S. top-forty pop chart songs. There's nothing wrong at all with this, but our desire to "sanctify" mainstream culture betrays our attitude: that the world is something we should withdraw from.

We assume that "we" are right and that "they" are wrong. And, of course, if all we ever hear are Christian voices giving Christian opinions on the world beyond the Church, then we are bound to take up the party line, believing that whatever is not overtly for Christ must, by definition, be against Him. Interestingly enough, as we retreat to be surrounded by none but our own, we mirror much of what has gone on in the gay scene: with its own pubs, clubs, holidays, and media.

But, of course, this is like trying to paint an intricate watercolor with a six-inch decorator's brush. It's way too clumsy, and the true picture is far more detailed and complex. We don't all sign up for the "hate the world/love the church" side of things, but in some ways we are all influenced to a greater or lesser extent by the general tide that pulls us away from engagement with mainstream culture, and particularly mainstream people. We might not be rampant fans of all things Christian, tuning our radios in to nothing but Christian stations, reading nothing but Christian books, and allowing ourselves the odd act of rebellion by watching *The Lion King*, but the attitudes filter down nevertheless.

Take social justice. I remember having a chat with the guy who later became my best man. He has always felt that church and Christianity are largely irrelevant to him. I was ranting on about how excited I was about the need for Christians to get involved with issues of poverty and so on. I'd been going some time when I realized he wasn't happy.

"You Christians think you've got the monopoly on good works, don't you?" he asked.

I was stunned. He was right. I shut up. A light had come on, and I realized that yes, I had believed that bread from a Christian was a better gift than bread from a Muslim. How terrible an attitude, how conceited and arrogant. "A starving belly has no ears to hear," goes the saying, but in my mind, acts of justice were performed not to feed or to uphold the rights of the oppressed, but to show what a good Christian I was. It's a return to the old idea of treating others as targets for Christian mission rather than people loved by God. This idea that we are the choice cuts, that we are God's premium selection through which all His best work is done stretches even further. It molds our attitudes to contemporary culture, our view of other people's worth to the value of work outside the Church and the importance of honing a faith that works out among a non-church environment. After all, if we are God's best, His chosen vehicle through which He only ever works, then what need is there for us to respect those who aren't?

Or take the idea of limited atonement. For many, evangelism can feel like an almost pointless task as—so the logic goes—those who are going to be saved have already been selected. This came up for me one lunch time at the school Christian Union where a youth worker was drafted in to give a talk. "You're all special," he told us. "You've been selected as ambassadors for God, and your task is to search out the others who also have their names written in the book of life, separating them from the ones who don't." Of course, this appealed to my view of things nicely, especially as I was in the middle of a long-range surveillance project, listening in on conversations and logging swearwords in my [Called To] account book.

This youth worker was not alone in his viewpoint, and I've met plenty of others who have grasped hold of the idea in some way. It might not be the full-on fervor of standing on street corners and proclaiming a life of eternal torture and punishment for all who don't happen to be in the club, but it can be traced to a desire to keep church topped up with the *right* people speaking the *right* language. "We are His people," we sing out loud, with the silent second line reading: "and it's really quite nice left like that."

The Effects of Our Self-Loathing

OK, so self-loathing might be going a bit far, but for many the lack of a true and accurate picture of how God feels about us does more than simply impact our own spiritual lives. It reaches out and can become clear for all, so much so that our claims of "good news" are totally undermined. "It doesn't matter if we all die," sang the Cure as it kicked off its album *Pornography*. Unless you were a fan of Captain Bob and his eye-linered crew, you had to work pretty hard to get past so bleak a beginning.

We take on board the apocalyptic language of the Bible and claim it as an assurance of imminent destruction. We love all "the sky will darken" language that appears there, and often apply it literally to our own situation. But as N.T. Wright points out in *The Challenge of Jesus*, Jesus' brief public career shows that He believed that both Israel and the world would be delivered salvation and justice through His own life, work, and ultimately death.

> This idea of the plan being unveiled is, again, character-istically Jewish, and Jesus' contemporaries had developed a highly complex way of talking about it. They used imagery, often lurid and spectacular, drawn from the Scriptures, to talk about things that were happening in the public world, the world of politics and society, and to give those happenings their theological meanings.
>
> Thus instead of saying "Babylon is going to fall, and this will be like a cosmic collapse," Isaiah said, "the sun will be darkened, the moon will not give its light, and the stars will be falling from heaven." (p. 21)

So that's a bit of a shame really, isn't it? Christianity is so much more *challenging* when we can draw on the idea that the whole earth is about to be consumed in the fire of God's judgment. It feels as if we believe that God just can't wait to be rid of this filthy world, us included. As soon as He gets around to it, He'll be dumping it in the trash and starting over with a whole new earth, populated solely by the handful of Christians who will keep quiet and not bother Him too much in the coming eons.

But if humanity is so fallen, if we really are so filthy with our sin, if Eve's apple tasting has tainted us all for the rest of time, why would God love us? Why would Jesus have died on the cross? Why would so much pain have been endured to establish a way of helping us find the right track?

What we can find ourselves left with is something way short of godly perfection. When others look at us, the sight that greets them not only helps them conclude that knowing God makes you miserable, but that there's little point in getting involved themselves. But as with everything in life, the key is finding the balance. Just knowing the truth is not enough, especially with regard to the twin extremes of godly love and godly judgment. It can almost appear that they are in conflict, that they cancel each other out. But digging deeper will help reveal a stronger, more complex truth, and if we can begin to grasp that, to understand more about what God really does think of the world, we will stand a much better chance of presenting the truth in a far more authentic way.

What Does the Bible Say About Premium Selection?

God chose the Israelites, right? So that means that in God's league, they were top of the class, yes? They were chosen to spread the Word because they were the best qualified at kicking foreign butt, is that it? No. In fact the Israelites were the weakest bunch around, as Deuteronomy points out: "For you are a people holy to the Lord your God. The Lord your God has chosen you out of all the peoples on the face of the earth to be his people, his treasured possession. The Lord did not set his affection on you and choose you because you were more numerous than other peoples, for you were the fewest of all peoples" (Deut. 7:6-7).

And it wasn't just because He felt sorry for them, either. In selecting the weakest, God was making clear exactly who was to get the credit for their blessed life. While the Israelites experienced God's grace and favor, it was very much in spite of what they had done rather than because of it. What's more, God didn't just choose the Israelites in order for them to keep it cozy between them. Here's a lineup that explains the full extent of God's plan:

- "Because he loved your forefathers and chose their descendants after them, he brought you out of Egypt by his Presence and his great strength" (Deut. 4:37-37).

- "For kings and all those in authority, that we may live peaceful and quiet lives in all godliness and holiness. This is good, and pleases God our Savior, who wants all men to be saved and to come to a knowledge of the truth" (1 Tim. 2:2-4).

- "'I will surely bless you and make your descendants as numerous as the stars in the sky and as the sand on the seashore. Your descendants will take possession of the cities of their enemies, and through your offspring all nations on earth will be blessed, because you have obeyed me'" (Gen. 22:17-18).

- "Your descendants will be like the dust of the earth, and you will spread out to the west and to the east, to the north and to the south. All peoples on earth will be blessed through you and your offspring" (Gen. 28:14).

God "wants all men to be saved ... all nations blessed ... all people blessed" and was prepared to use the weakest bunch around to do it. Not only does that give us a clear picture of the power of God, but of the goodness of His heart as well. As mentioned before, God uses the individual to bless the universal, the one nation for the rest of the world. Make sense? The creator of man uses that creation as a tool for all of them.

We have plenty in common with the Israelites, and not just in the fact that we Christians know the blessing and love of God. A weakness for introspection and arrogance crops up throughout the Old Testament, nowhere more so than in the later prophets.

The story of Jonah reveals the true extent of the Israelites' decay within after years of wandering away from God and living life on their own terms with a taste for both religious separatism and kings that made them feel important. Remember the story about Jonah in the whale? It's more than just a Sunday school story, and it combines with the harsh messages of Amos and Hosea that warn the Israelites of the dangers of their smug complacency.

The story of Jonah is set against the backdrop of Israel's troubles with Assyria, one of Israel's greatest and most powerful enemies. They were in need of a severe godly kicking (according to Israelite thought, that is), and the prospect of taking the five-hundred-mile hike to take them the Word of God was not exactly Jonah's idea of fun. We all know the story from here—Jonah does a bunk and hitches a ride on a ship heading in the opposite direction; the ship hits a storm; Jonah finally wises up to the fact that the storm is God's judgment on him, so he persuades the crew to chuck him overboard where he gets swallowed by a whale, feels rough, and eventually agrees to do the right thing.

But for a man who has just faced death due to his dislike of the inhabitants of Nineveh, Jonah remains superbly annoyed, mumbling something about "those who cling to worthless idols forfeit the grace that could be theirs" (Jon. 2:8). Still, the thumb in his mouth doesn't completely prevent him from being used by God, and he makes his way there:

> On the first day, Jonah started into the city. He proclaimed: "Forty more days and Nineveh will be overturned." The Ninevites believed God. They declared a fast, and all of them, from the greatest to the least, put on sackcloth. When the news reached the king of Nineveh,

he rose from his throne, took off his royal robes, covered himself with sackcloth and sat down in the dust. Then he issued a proclamation in Nineveh: "By the decree of the king and his nobles: Do not let any man or beast, herd or flock, taste anything; do not let them eat or drink." (Jon. 3:4-7)

For a book about a prophetic mission, this one hardly gives the prophecy a lot of room. I mean, just one line is hardly up there with Isaiah's free-flow. Jonah certainly didn't try to argue the Ninevites into submission as the solitary "forty more days and Nineveh will be overturned" is yet another hint that he feels that these pesky foreigners are not worth saving.

Amazingly enough, Jonah's almost pathetic window of opportunity is more than enough for God to work through, and both the people and the king are prepared for an immediate turnaround. The result? "When God saw what they did and how they turned from their evil ways, he had compassion and did not bring upon them the destruction he had threatened" (Jon. 3:10).

But Jonah was greatly displeased and became angry. He prayed to the Lord, "O Lord, is this not what I said when I was still at home? That is why I was so quick to flee to Tarshish. I knew that you are a gracious and compassionate God, slow to anger and abounding in love, a God who relents from sending calamity. Now, O Lord, take away my life, for it is better for me to die than to live." But the Lord replied, "Have you any right to be angry?" Jonah went out and sat down at a place east of the city. (Jon. 4:1-5)

Jealousy, racial hatred, sour grapes—call it what you like, the simple truth is that Jonah could not stand the thought of God having compassion on His enemies. By wishing to die, Jonah throws the miracle that God had performed in saving his own life back in God's face. It all gets summed up with the story about the vine and the worm: the Lord grows the vine to protect Jonah, but then sends a worm to destroy it and a scorching wind to intensify the heat on his head. Has he any right to be angry at the forces of nature? No. Has he any right to be angry with the will of God? No. Has he any right to claim that the universe revolves around either him or his people? No.

The sin of separation, the worm that eats into the vine of the Church and threatens to undo the provision and shelter that we are supposed to offer, is contrary to the will of God. Believing that salvation makes us separate is a dangerous path to walk, that God's heart beats for a select bunch more than it does for any other is rubbish. God's heart beats for all—a fact which also lets the air out of the "God Hates Me" tire.

"I urge, then, first of all, that requests, prayers, intercession and thanksgiving be made for everyone—for kings and all those in authority, that we may live peaceful and quiet lives in all godliness and holiness. This is good, and pleases God our Savior, who wants all men to be saved and to come to a knowledge of the truth" (1 Tim. 2:1-4).

What Does the Bible Say About Having the Monopoly on Good Works?

Believing that God works solely through Christians is an indefensible position. Take Joshua, for example. Prior to his arrival in Canaan, he sends out two spies with the mission of checking out the state of play in the enemy city of Jericho. They find shelter in the house of Rahab, who is not only a resident in the enemy city, but a prostitute living, like many other outcasts, quite literally on the edge of society in her house built into the wall. Not only does she offer them shelter, she helped them escape, scammed with the authorities, and told them the safest route home. Not bad for a woman. And a prostitute. And an enemy.

This theme of God working in mysterious ways is picked up later as Joshua prepares to lead the army on to victory.

> Now when Joshua was near Jericho, he looked up and saw a man standing in front of him with a drawn sword in his hand. Joshua went up to him and asked, "Are you for us or for our enemies?" "Neither," he replied, "but as commander of the army of the Lord I have now come." Then Joshua fell facedown to the ground in reverence, and asked him, "What message does my Lord have for his servant?" The commander of the Lord's army replied, "Take off your sandals, for the place where you are standing is holy." And Joshua did so. (Josh. 5:13-15)

Joshua, focused on the battle and with the whole nation backed up behind him, is understandably a tad nervous. But his question of the suddenly appearing swordsman brings up more than just a case of butterflies in the stomach. Whose side is he on, he asks, understandably enough, but he has failed to comprehend the truth of the situation. It's God's battle not Joshua's. This isn't a case of God pitching in to help the Israelites crush the Canaanites; it's another step in the establishing of God's kingdom, another move to bring salvation to the world. The real question is whether Joshua is on God's side, whether he is fighting the Lord's battle or his own.

Fast forward a few years and you come up against the stories of Ezra and Nehemiah, men who worked hard to re-establish in Jerusalem the captives from Judah who had been exiled in Babylon.

Ezra kicks off thus: "In the first year of Cyrus king of Persia, in order to fulfil the word of the Lord spoken by Jeremiah, the Lord moved the heart of Cyrus king of Persia to make a proclamation throughout his realm and to put it in writing" (Ezra 1:1).

Not bad for a non God-fearing foreigner. And we can be sure that he was both of those by taking a look at what the Lord says in Isaiah:

> Who says of Cyrus, "He is my shepherd and will accomplish all that I please; he will say of Jerusalem, 'Let it be rebuilt,' and of the temple, 'Let its foundations be laid.'" This is what the Lord says to his anointed, to Cyrus, whose right hand I take hold of to subdue nations before him and to strip kings of their armor, to open doors before him so that gates will not be shut: I will go before you and will level the mountains; I will break down gates of bronze and cut through bars of iron. I will give you the treasures of darkness, riches stored in secret places, so that you may know that I am the Lord, the God of Israel, who summons you by name. For the sake of Jacob my servant, of Israel my chosen, I summon you by name and bestow on you a title of honor, though you do not acknowledge me. I am the Lord, and there is no other; apart from me there is no God. I will strengthen you, though you have not acknowledged me, so that from the rising of the sun to the place of its setting men may know there is none besides me. I am the Lord, and there is no other. I form the light and create darkness, I bring

prosperity and create disaster; I, the Lord, do all these things. (Isa. 44:28-45:7)

Later we read that Darius, Cyrus' successor also supported the rebuilding project, as did King Xerxes. Not only did he put up with the bare-faced cheek of young Nehemiah, but he also put his hand in his pocket and splashed the cash for this foreign servant's reconstruction project.

> "If it pleases the king and if your servant has found favor in his sight, let him send me to the city in Judah where my fathers are buried so that I can rebuild it." Then the king, with the queen sitting beside him, asked me, "How long will your journey take, and when will you get back?" It pleased the king to send me; so I set a time. I also said to him, "If it pleases the king, may I have letters to the governors of Trans-Euphrates, so that they will provide me safe-conduct until I arrive in Judah? And may I have a letter to Asaph, keeper of the king's forest, so he will give me timber to make beams for the gates of the citadel by the temple and for the city wall and for the residence I will occupy?" And because the gracious hand of my God was upon me, the king granted my requests. So I went to the governors of Trans-Euphrates and gave them the king's letters. The king had also sent army officers and cavalry with me. When Sanballat the Horonite and Tobiah the Ammonite official heard about this, they were very much disturbed that someone had come to promote the welfare of the Israelites. (Neh. 2:5-10)

Finally, let's move on to the New Testament where Jesus addresses the members of the synagogue. Reading from Isaiah 61, He makes the boldest of claims: that He is the messiah. Pre-empting the inevitable jibes—"Oh, but you're Joe's lad ... you can't be the messiah ... I've known you since you were a child"—He launches into a speech that reveals even more of God's ability to work through the most unusual of vehicles:

> "I tell you the truth," he continued, "no prophet is accepted in his hometown. I assure you that there were many widows in Israel in Elijah's time, when the sky was shut for three and a half years and there was a severe famine throughout the land. Yet Elijah was not sent to any of them, but to a widow in Zarephath in the region of Sidon. And there were many in Israel with leprosy in the time of Elisha the prophet, yet not one of them was cleansed—only Naaman the Syrian." All the people in the synagogue were furious when they heard this. They got up, drove him out of the town, and took him to the brow of the hill on which the town was built, in order to throw him down the cliff. But he walked right through the crowd and went on his way. (Luke 4:24-30)

Why so strong a reaction? Because Jesus was reminding them that God works through non-Jews: the widow from Sidon and Naaman the Syrian. God works through the individual, for the benefit of the universal; and the individual—or so it would appear—could be absolutely anyone. You see, it's God's battle not ours. We're not here to select the team, to field our best players in the hope that they will somehow produce a better result. This is God's game, the one in which all the skill, talent, inspiration, and goals come directly from Him. Do Christians have the monopoly on the good works? No. Does God? Yes indeed.

What Does the Bible Say About How God Speaks?

If we're still feeling puffed up and special, it's worth reminding ourselves that in God's battle He speaks to and through whom He likes. Wise men following the star to Bethlehem? They were probably Persians keen on a bit of astrology—that's astrology as in horoscopes and star charts rather than astronomy as in star gazing. Balaam's donkey in Numbers 22? The ass speaks and brings Balaam to his senses after a string of offenses. As well as trying to line his pockets out of God's Word, he encouraged the Israelites to worship idols. Not only did God use a donkey to turn him around spiritually, but he went on to use him to encourage the Israelites. But if we're after a tasty treat around the theme of hearing God, the search is up when we come to Gideon.

The story begins with the Israelites in the middle of a familiar cycle: wandering away from God, in trouble with their enemies, and in need of serious help. Who gets the job? Why, little Gideon. And who—apart from the Israelites—does he have to sort out? Some tricky customers known as the Midianites. There may not have been many of them, but they were a sneaky bunch, perhaps the first to use camels as part of their guerrilla warfare tactics. What made it even tougher was the fact that these thugs were distant relatives of the Israelites, as they were descendants from Abraham's second wife, Keturah.

So Gideon is scared, unsure about the way things should be. He—like us—wants confirmation and asks God to speak to him. There's all that stuff with fleeces, where he asks God to confirm certain details by making the ground wet and the fleece dry in the morning, and the other way around the next day. Petty-minded and lacking in faith, Gideon reduced the Almighty to little more than a cheap magician. God whittles down his army from thirty-two thousand men to three hundred and underlines the question in red ink: Do you trust me? Then something wonderful happens:

> Now the camp of Midian lay below him in the valley.
> During that night the Lord said to Gideon, "Get up, go
> down against the camp, because I am going to give it into
> your hands. If you are afraid to attack, go down to the
> camp with your servant Purah and listen to what they
> are saying. Afterward, you will be encouraged to attack
> the camp." So he and Purah his servant went down to the
> outposts of the camp. The Midianites, the Amalekites
> and all the other eastern peoples had settled in the valley,
> thick as locusts. Their camels could no more be counted
> than the sand on the seashore. Gideon arrived just as a
> man was telling a friend his dream. "I had a dream," he
> was saying. "A round loaf of barley bread came tumbling
> into the Midianite camp. It struck the tent with such
> force that the tent overturned and collapsed." His friend
> responded, "This can be nothing other than the sword
> of Gideon son of Joash, the Israelite. God has given the
> Midianites and the whole camp into his hands." When
> Gideon heard the dream and its interpretation, he wor-
> shiped God. He returned to the camp of Israel and called
> out, "Get up! The Lord has given the Midianite camp
> into your hands." (Judg. 8:9-15)

We know that dreams and interpretations are special things throughout the Bible, particularly in the Old Testament. There are many cases of non-believers having a dream and men of God being given the interpretation, with Joseph perhaps the most fa-mous. But this is a first: a non-follower of God having the dream, and another non-follower having the interpretation. And it's correct. Heck, God even tells Gideon to listen to their conversation as he will receive encouragement about the divine plan.

The whole thing smacks of God's mighty power. A mini-loaf of bread made out of second-rate materials is enough to crush a tent. A pathetically small army whips butt on an almighty scale. A frightened, untrusting man gets to be at the front of the move of God. A couple of enemies—soon to end up dead—are used by God as His mouthpiece. It's almost too much to take in, but take it in we must: God works how, when, and through whomever He likes in order to achieve His purpose.

Our preconceived ideas of how God speaks are often bound up in our perception of status and superiority. After all, to acknowledge that God could use others as tools is to acknowledge that we are but tools ourselves. This level of democracy does not sit easy with us, especially when we're struggling to define the difference between our spirituality and the crystal-wearing, feng shui practicing contemporaries: we must be different, we must be better. But this is God's battle, and we are merely part of the team. And who are we fighting? The injustice, sin, and oppression that are the result of a world turned from God. Sometimes the battle is out there with elements of the world that are living contrary to God—the oppressors themselves. But at other times the fight takes place on home turf, against our own sin; our desire to hold on to God's blessing for ourselves, our self-conceit that we are better than others, our self-delusion that God only speaks to and through us. Sometimes the battle is in us.

Is There No Difference Between Us?

OK, so, point taken about our tendency to be combative without compassion, self-deluded, awkward about admitting failure, and unwilling to step down from our podium. But am I suggesting that we sell up and move down pantheism avenue? Are we to believe that God is everywhere, in everyone allowing them to do whatever takes their fancy? Is there no judgment, no line in the sand?

When I was a fresh-faced and earnest twenty-one-year-old, I turned up for my first assignment working on a Christian magazine. It involved turning up to the Greenbelt festival of that summer and interviewing as many bands as I could. The one that caught my eye was a mainstream act that was simply there for the chance of a little extra exposure. It wasn't exactly big time, and it definitely wasn't at one with the Christian values that underpinned the festival, and I loved the guys.

I asked them what they thought about God. Did they believe in Him, in Jesus and the cross?

"The way I see it," said one, "is that religion is like one big mountain. There are many ways up it, but all routes lead to the same point at the top. Yeah, I believe in Jesus, but I believe in Buddha and Krishna too. All of them, men of God."

I was delighted. This was exactly the sort of thing that the magazine needed to publish, helping young Christians to break away from the ghetto mentality and developing a far more open and inclusive approach to spirituality. I even got the page designed and submitted it to the editorial board to be published. They took one look and, quite rightly, threw it out.

Part of me had been caught up by the glamour of meeting in person a couple of C-list celebrities, but there was another part that wanted to believe that God was inclusive. OK, so I may have been dumb, but at the time I was finding the issue of judgment a hard aspect of the Gospel to come to grips with. If God was love, why did He have to say "no" to people? What's more, in this day and age, being tough and hard-line about anything relating to morality is so passé, so 1950s, that it's simply not done.

Incidentally, this wasn't the only time I felt the pangs of cultural embarrassment. Reading a music magazine, I saw a piece responding to a letter about the attempts of Christian bands to get into the charts. The editorial was banging on about how the writer couldn't stand Christians who preached niceness and love. According to the writer, this was pure hypocrisy as everyone knew that the Bible was bigoted and homophobic. "I have much more respect for those that come out and declare themselves such fascists." Gulp. Was that really the only way I could be? A hard-line moron who preached hatred and damnation?

Perhaps they are a both a little too extreme for you, a little too ridiculous to relate to. But the tension of finding the right take on the state of the human soul has been bothering people for years. Calvin mulled over the idea of whether humanity is irrevocably flawed, whether the extent of sin has left all bankrupt from birth. But what does that say about the fact that God created man "in His image"? If a conclusion can be arrived at in so short a space, let's leave it at this: We are made in God's image, and as such, we all bear the marks of our creator. But those marks, that sparkle of God-ness can become dirtied by sin and the state of mankind. Yet despite the extent of the dirt, the true image of God can never be fully wiped out.

An evangelist I heard of puts it this way: He takes out a newly made, crisp fifty-dollar bill from his wallet. "Who wants it?" he asks. Pretty much everyone in the room puts up a hand. Then he messes the bill up. He treads on it. He spits on it. Smears mud on it. Throws it about and generally makes it look a lot less crisp and shiny than before. "Who wants it?" he asks. People still put up their hands. The line? That's what we're like—dirtied, sullied, abused, corrupted, taken away from the glory that once we started with and reduced to a pale reflection. But we're still worth the same. Then he gives the bill away.

What Did People See When They Looked at Jesus?

If we're wondering what people should see when they look at us, it's probably wise to do a bit of head-scratching over the whole issue of what people saw when they looked at Jesus. And seeing as how we've already mentioned Jonah, why not look where Jesus joined the dots between Himself and the moody fish-mouth chap of old.

> Then some of the Pharisees and teachers of the law said to him, "Teacher, we want to see a miraculous sign from you." He answered, "A wicked and adulterous generation asks for a miraculous sign! But none will be given it except the sign of the prophet Jonah. For as Jonah was three days and three nights in the belly of a huge fish, so the Son of Man will be three days and three nights in the heart of the earth. The men of Nineveh will stand up at the judgment with this generation and condemn it; for they repented at the preaching of Jonah, and now one greater than Jonah is here." (Matt. 12:38-41)

One greater than Jonah, certainly at first glance one of the less impressive claims made by Jesus; Jonah wasn't exactly a hero, now was he? But there is more than meets the eye. They both came from the same area, with Nazareth about one hour's walk from Jonah's pad at Gath-hepher. What's more, Jonah is the only Old Testament prophet with whom Jesus directly aligns Himself.

In asking for a nice juicy sign with which to be impressed and start believing in His identity, the Pharisees were trying to bend Jesus in a direction that He didn't want to go. This wasn't the stubbornness of Jonah but the supreme wisdom of a man who came to remix the ingredients of power in a truly revolutionary way.

And Jesus really was greater than Jonah. Jonah complained about being "banished" from God's sight, Jesus cried "my God, my God, why have you forsaken me?" (Matt. 27:46). Where Jonah was facing death, Jesus actually died. Where Jonah escaped death, Jesus came back to life. Where Jonah begrudgingly agreed to help the miserable scum known as the Ninevites, "those who cling to worthless idols forfeit the grace" (Jon. 2:8), Jesus went through an agonizing death because of His compassion. Jonah lacked compassion; Jesus died for it. Jonah's public face was obstinate, rude, uncaring, and self-serving; Jesus' was caring, considerate, self-sacrificing, patient, and honest. Where Jonah delivered the judgment, Jesus combined it with the salvation.

You see, Jesus changed everything. In dying on the cross and rising again, He put a marker in all time, answering those who called for a sign in the most dramatic way possible. The cross changes everything for humankind, drawing a line in the sand. It lets us know that our sin is worth death. Our sin caused Jesus to take on the ultimate punishment. It says, "Because of you, I have died." It makes us all guilty, demanding that we all acknowledge just how far short from God's standard of perfection we fall.

But it offers something else too: an eternal "yes." It is the sign of acceptance, of victory over the power of sin that threatens to dirty our view of God time and time again. It says that all are welcome, that in dying for everyone, Jesus made accessibility to God an option for all people. It says that we are all worth saving, all called the children of God.

This is the balance that we need to find in our lives. The awareness of our own sin combined with the joy of Christ's victory over it. The grief at what we have done mixed with the celebration over the part that He has played. The understanding that judgment affects us all, but that salvation reaches just as far. It is the most selfless act ever performed. It is the victory at the heart of God's battle.

What do people really see when they look at us? All too often we seem more like Jonah than Jesus. We focus on our own frustrations and pains, view the work of God through the lens of our own selfishness. Serve the poor? I'm too tired. Show someone a glimpse of God's compassion? I'd rather not, thanks. Help bring people back to God? But they're sinners, and I don't like them, and they're doing all the wrong things, and I'd really rather that they didn't come into church and spoil it all for me 'cause I've just about got it how I like it. But do we really want to be the ones who said "no" to God? Do we really want to be the ones who fought our own battle instead of His?

"Christianity is for all. Yep, even the ones who don't look right."

5

What Does the World Look Like to Me?

The Importance of the Sight Test

It's 1984. I'm eleven years old, and I'm crouched on the patio at home with a sledge hammer by my side. In front lie the shattered remains of my music collection; reels of tape curl themselves around the shards of plastic. I have just spent twenty-three minutes struggling to pick up the hammer and let it fall down onto such musical treats as Barry Manilow's *Love Songs* and The Beatles' *Ballads*. Why? Because they are evil. Thanks to the grace of God, I have recently been made aware of the need for constant vigilance whenever listening to any music other than traditional church hymns. I have discovered the shocking truth that Satan is firmly embedded in the driver's seat and uses a frightening array of techniques to corrupt the pure souls of the world. And so I had no choice. The Beatles smoked dope, so they were obviously part of Lucifer's plan. And Barry Manilow? He had to go because of the lust demon that was so obviously at large within his soul.

*

It's now 1987. I'm fifteen years old, and I'm staring up at a curvaceous honey in red and black lycra. She is dancing on the podium in a way that has me transfixed, but this is no club. It's 9:16 a.m. We're at a Christian festival, and this is church. Around me are a few hundred people letting themselves go as the tunes are loud and harsh and the video screen shows moving images of cloudscapes, tides, and sunsets. This is church as I've never seen it before, but as far as myself and the couple of friends who are standing next to me are concerned, there's only one aspect we're focusing on. "Oh, thank you, God, for making women" we murmur as she does a move I think I once saw in a Bond movie. We've heard rumored that one of the aims of the service is to "reclaim the erotic back for God," and I'm hoping for an awful lot more of the same when we get back home to sleepy Chorleywood.

*

The world outside the Church can take on different tones and hues for each of us, and my attitudes have shifted plenty over the years. From the paranoid psychosis of believing that even elevator music held the power to pepper my soul with demons to longing for the church to introduce naked mud wrestling into the order of service, my view of the world has been in need of serious help. Whether it's the short-sighted inability to see any good beyond the Church or the long-sighted tendency to blur the edges between Church and world, this naked Christian needs glasses.

It's All About Focus

For many of us, the world at times can seem troubling and repulsive or appealing and alluring. In truth, both positions are right; there are elements of good and bad all around us, but the key to establishing a healthy way of looking at the world is learning the importance of that word *elements*. The name of the game is neither to lock ourselves away in fear or to stroll away from God's heart in ignorance. The name of the game is getting the world in focus.

They're Out to Get Me!

Suffering from short-sightedness means that our view of the world at large is forced into a distorted image of degradation, decay, and general moral decline. The chances are that what will come to mind for some of us—particularly members of the older generations—when we think of the world beyond the Church are images of drug dens, swearing, and gimp masks, despite the fact life on our own doorstep might suggest otherwise. We often think of the media as the window through which we can get the clearest picture, but when looking for an example of "how the world is" we pick *Trainspotting* over *Chicken Run*, Eminem over Ronan Keeting, Irvine Welsh over Nick Hornby. We opt for the scariest, brashest, most ungodly elements to define culture. Why? Because (as Clive Calver describes) the legacy handed to us is one of fear: "Many of us have genuinely had to bury our heads in the sand because we just could not cope with a syndrome of change which resembled a railway locomotive hurtling brakeless down a steep gradient with a hairpin bend at the bottom! Youth culture has proved to be too horrendous, and we've had to turn our heads in distaste."

Perhaps we're keen to hold on to some of this attitude of fear. After all, if we admit that there may not be a case for sheer terror at the thought of worldly engagement, then we smash the clay feet of our belief that God wants us separate, that the world is dirty, and that we should have nothing to do with it.

I'm Out to Show Them!

When it's more an issue of long-sightedness, then we move to the other extreme of the trap of failing to distinguish between what is and what is not of God. The lines of behavior and personal morality can easily become blurred as we struggle hard against the repressive nature of the ghetto mentality. We long to see God in everything. We long to view Him as busting out of the narrow confines of religion and redefining everything. God is omnipotent and omnipresent, and anything that holds us back is brushed aside as stale religion. But it can become a competition to put a mild spin of interpretation on anything, and we become like art critics standing in front of an obscure piece of modernist confusion. It's a classic postmodern approach, as we deconstruct the world around us, saying that all that matters is the interpretation. In line with the rest of this movement, we edge away from the sticky absolutes, the rights and wrongs of the faith. If you want to show your credibility, just mention that Hamlet is all about genetic cloning, Damien Hirst is about urban angst, and Scooby Doo is a powerful interpretation of the ministry of the Holy Spirit. With that under our belts, we can set our sights on really teaching those narrow-minded bigots a thing or two, reaching the dizzy heights of finding God in Eminem, *Trainspotting*, and gimp masks too.

But a long-sighted view is not all about frustrated reaction against the repressive nature of the Christian ghetto. As we'll come onto later, there is a great need for us to widen our field of vision and perceive God at work in the beautiful minutiae of everyday life. But this needs to be tempered with both a greater understanding of what God's fingerprints look like and an honest appraisal of our motives for embracing more than the established norm. It doesn't take a genius to work out that my motives for wishing erotic worship to be a central part of the midweek church meeting were anything other than a stirring in my loins. But loin-stirring can be a powerful feeling, one that makes objective thought kind of difficult. It took a cold shower of reality from my youth leader to sort me out. So, at the risk of sounding like a broken record, we find ourselves the audience of a familiar song: the need for balance, the imperative of focus.

Can Short-Sightedness Be Helped?

There is more than one type of error that can prevent us from seeing the world as God intended, and the couple of myths that are associated with the closed mindset have both fed off selective passages of the Bible. But this type of approach to the Bible simply won't do. It might be more enjoyable, less hard work, and easier to mold to suit the reader's wishes, but taking a verse here and a verse there does God's Word a grave injustice. We treat the Bible like a greeting card, one with a tidy—if a little pithy—message inside. Read it in three seconds and everything's lovely. And like greeting cards, we often put it down after reading with a sigh, a mumble of "Aah, that's nice," and carry on with our lives. The idea of taking in the context of any particular passage, of learning to appreciate the Bible on its many levels—from historical to inspirational, prophetic to allegorical, poetic to factual—goes against the grain. In fact, so keen are we on adopting the feed-me-quick-and-feed-me-now characteristics of mainstream culture, there's even a program you can load onto your computer called Bible Bingo. Each day it will deliver a choice morsel designed to lift your soul and feed your march heavenward. It's all very well if you get Psalm 97:12: "Rejoice in the Lord, you who are righteous, and praise his holy name." Or if you happen to be a male landscape gardener and you turn up Proverbs 5:18: "May your fountain be blessed, and may you rejoice in the wife of your youth." But what about if you get Ezekiel 23:21: "So you longed for the lewdness of your youth, when in Egypt your bosom was caressed and your young breasts fondled." Or the bizarre sounding Leviticus 9:21: "Aaron waved the breasts and the right thigh before the Lord as a wave offering, as Moses commanded." Of course, Bible Bingo will give you none of these ones as it only selects the nice bits of the Bible. This is Bible Lite, Bible Purée, an unappealing mush that gives no hint of flavor, nutrition, or the chef Himself.

But we digress. The first myth that has taken root is that the world is somehow evil. Whether it's the misinformed belief that violent crime is on the up or the assumption that the devil is fully in control of anything that doesn't belong in church, the underlying foundations are the same. If it isn't "Christian," then it's of the devil. I heard about a couple who had lived without a TV for years, staunchly resisting the infection of worldly images and themes into their safe haven called home. Eventually their courage grew, and they felt ready to take the step of finally purchasing one. Having made their selection they returned home and awaited the delivery. Imagine their horror when the TV arrived and the cardboard packaging proclaimed the slogan: "Bringing the world into your home." They wanted neither the world nor the TV and sent it back straightaway.

Pure paranoia plucked at random from out of the air? Not quite, as the New Testament appears to offer a gentle prod in precisely that direction:

"You adulterous people, don't you know that friendship with the world is hatred toward God? Anyone who chooses to be a friend of the world becomes an enemy of God" (James 4:4).

Taken on its own and without an attempt at understanding it, this verse could be used to back up some of the most outrageous of positions. Surely that bit about friendship with the world making you an enemy of God makes it clear that the world is evil? But it's confusing though, isn't it? I mean, I always thought that we were supposed to be friends with people? How can James say that it's suddenly off limits?

The truth is out there in the surrounding verses. Here (and in James 1:27) "the world" does not refer to creation. Instead it indicates a state of rebellion against God. There's a similar thing going on in 1 John 2:15, where the writer tells the audience "do not love the world or anything to do with the world." Thankfully, he goes on to define "the world," or more specifically, the specific elements in it that we should avoid: "the cravings of sinful man, the lust of his eyes and the boasting of what he has and does" (1 John 2:16). It is this sin, these acts of rebellion against the holiness of God that we should be avoiding. Take a look back at James' words, and it's easy to see that yes, we should love God more than rebelling against Him, but that doesn't mean we should be making ourselves a cozy little ghetto in which to hide away from the big, bad world. James knows that Jesus' message was all about getting involved, both with God and with the world, as the verses that follow clearly show.

> Submit yourselves, then, to God. Resist the devil, and he will flee from you. Come near to God and he will come near to you. Wash your hands, you sinners, and purify your hearts, you doubleminded. Grieve, mourn and wail. Change your laughter to mourning and your joy to gloom. Humble yourselves before the Lord, and he will lift you up. Brothers, do not slander one another.

Anyone who speaks against his brother or judges him speaks against the law and judges it. When you judge the law, you are not keeping it, but sitting in judgment on it. (James 4:7-11)

Christianity, in that sense, is action based: submit, resist, come near, wash, purify ... look at all those commands for us to do something, each one helping us to have a full-on relationship with God. It's not even about getting out there and kicking off a few fights, whipping some heathen booty as we flex our spiritual pecs. God's plan is different; once we have truly submitted, washed, purified, and all that, we will know our place is not to judge others—we should leave that to God.

Instead of fodder for hiding under the bedsheet of religion while the scary ghouls of culture run riot in the dark, the party line becomes this: Pursue God, live your life for His affirmation not the world's, and learn to serve.

The other myth doing the rounds is the idea that God calls us to be separate. Whether it takes the form of avoiding anything other than "Christian" leisure pursuits or believing that talents can only really be used when the monthly paycheck comes from a Christian company, the pressure to withdraw can make life occasionally uninspiring and frequently claustrophobic.

The influences that have bred this myth can be found in many places. The feeling that the Church is the modern-day Israel can lead people to scoop up for themselves many of the words and prophecies that were given to the chosen people all those years ago. The commands not to marry people of other faiths or nationalities, the imperative to stick close to ritual and avoid any form of contamination spur us on to draw the wagons in around us and huddle up away from the unseen enemy.

This sense of the need to keep the outside world away from us goes hand in hand with the myth that the world is evil and that Christians are easy pickings for the devil. Much as it might inject an element of excitement into the proceedings, it is simply not true that God is in some way weaker than the devil. There is no evidence within the Bible to support such a claim, and while some Christians simply won't go near a mosque, temple, or pub for fear of encountering serious spiritual damage, Jesus' model of one who was happy to mix with sinners is a sound example of the strength of God's love. If there were a fifty-fifty chance of our being dragged off by a hoard of demons the minute we step off the holy ground of our local church, then yes, there might be an argument for staying put. But this fantasy worldview of salvation being a bit of a close run thing just cannot sit comfortably with a belief that Jesus both died and rose again. In that act is found the ultimate confirmation God is bigger than any opposing power, and as His children we too can share in the confidence that allows our interaction with a world that in places is far from ideal.

The real shocker about the "sanctified and separate" line of thinking is the way that it has been manipulated to line the pockets of a certain few. The growth in the Christian sales industry may not have been quite as phenomenal in the U.K. as it has in the United States, but in both markets there are people making a good deal of money out of a misreading of Scripture. I've got a copy of a Christian retailing magazine, a U.S. trade publication that I allow myself a sneak viewing only every so often. It makes me depressed: you see all those ads and editorials about how wonderful it is that a certain stuffed toy that looks vaguely like Richard Branson has become the market leader in Jesus dolls, or a glowing report on how WWJD products have now grossed x-million dollars. Anyone for turning over a few market stalls?

"Finally, brothers, whatever is true, whatever is noble, whatever is right, whatever is pure, whatever is lovely, whatever is admirable—if anything is excellent or praiseworthy—think about such things" (Phil. 4:8).

In the hands of the marketing man, this becomes the ultimate product plug: Don't even think about anything that is evil or ungodly; instead fill up on the pure spring that can only come from a Christian's work. It gets used to sell anything from clothing to music, builders to books. But is Paul really telling the readers to train their minds never to wander from the fish-stamped and sanctified? Isn't that a little difficult? The fact is that, yes, Paul is encouraging the readers to strive toward a more holy standard of living, but not by mental constipation and spiritual sedatives. The word *think* is used a lot in the letter to the Philippians, often to encourage the readers to keep their attitudes a certain way. Here a stronger word was used in the original Greek (*logizomai*), and it gives his words a little more oomph. Instead of it being about focus, Paul's encouragement is to put some serious energy into thinking about the very nature of godly behavior: "Whatever you have learned or received or heard from me, or seen in me—put it into practice. And the God of peace will be with you" (Phil. 4:9).

The verse that follows sheds even more light. Why should we be grappling with these concepts? To allow them to shape our behavior, to mold us into the type of Christians that we are supposed to be. The aim is not to merely develop a talent for mental manipulation, but to become—and I'm sorry if this sounds a bit cheesy and gag-worthy—better people.

But just lately, things seem to have been changing in the Church. We have been made aware of the changes going on in the mainstream culture that surrounds us all, have begun to feel a little less scared, and have been fired up on a desire to get involved. For many this is a positive step—learning about God's God-ness. But there is still a danger that the old myths could have an effect. Take Delirious?, for example. For a time the band's attempts at getting into the charts and playing in non-church venues were carried out under the banner of "invading the culture." This was perhaps an unfortunate choice of phrase. The band members themselves have always taken an unassuming and non-threatening approach to people with other beliefs, and far from wanting to pick a fight, they've been happy simply to make friends with those they've met. But perhaps it was the hangover from the myths that sparked such a combative line, as after all, "invading" does bring to mind images of fighting, enemies, right and wrong.

This football terrace mentality takes us away from Jesus' model that we see in the Gospels. Instead of turning up to repackage, reclaim, and rebrand any and everything that He came into contact with by force, Jesus did it differently. Through His choice of dining partners (women, sinners, enemies, and outcasts), Jesus preached radical acceptance and forgiveness.

How frustrating is it to try to explain some aspect of your faith to someone who simply refuses to listen? In fact, when the listener fails to even entertain the possibility that you might be right, he cannot be listening at all, right? Surely some degree of openness, some element of preparation to accept that the speaker may have something to teach is a key component of listening. If this is so, then it works the other way for us; can we really listen to others if we believe that they have nothing to teach us? This closed-mind is what makes politicians so infuriating to watch at cross-party debates, and it might be worth asking ourselves if there are a few tweaks that need to be made to our own inner ear. Of course, there are certain absolutes that the Christian can never throw away—the birth, death, and resurrection of Christ, the reality of judgment and salvation as well as the hope of eternal life and vitality of the Bible as God's revealed Word—but are we really so sure that we've got the rest of life sussed? As we saw in the previous chapter, God is not averse to speaking and working through the type of person who might not exactly make it up onto our festival platforms. Are we really so sure that we have not only the monopoly on the good works but on the wise words as well? Can the world beyond the Church teach us nothing of value? In the search for clear focus, we need to be able not only to hang on to the truths that have helped to make the Church strong, but to recognize the freedom that is ours to explore the breadth of how God works.

Can Long-Sightedness Be Helped?

Starting my second year at university was an odd time. I'd come back to Christianity during the previous summer and was facing challenges to my assumptions about how my faith worked on an almost daily basis. I was surrounded by good friends, none of them Christians. As far as I could tell, the only Christians around me were lifeless and stale, and the only thing that the Christian Union had done of note in the recent past was publish a leaflet that claimed AIDS was God's just punishment on a sinful life. Not surprisingly, I steered well clear, choosing to join a church twenty miles away.

My notebook is full of random thoughts and scribbled prayers, and embarrassing as it is to read now, it charts an up-and-down kind of year. One minute I'm writing about God's mighty plan for my life and my desire to change Egham in a single day, while the next I'm confessing yet another slip-up down at the student union with lil' Vinny, Smelly Dave, and too much time on our hands. But they aren't all confessions of alcohol-induced errors, as much of the time it seems like I'm battling between a desire to be normal and a desire to be holy. In my twisted logic, the only options I ever seemed to latch on to were becoming so heavily camouflaged a Christian that nobody could tell the difference between my pre- and post-conversion states or kicking into spiritual earnestness overdrive and freaking most people out quite considerably. On one of these up-turns, I thought it was about time I laid down the law regarding spiritual warfare for my two friends. To the gently stoned Vincent and Dave, a two-hour lecture on demonic possession, deliverance, and the realities of satanic influence was probably not quite what the doctor ordered. Some choice.

The Christian ghetto sits uncomfortably with many of us, and many peoples' desire to break out of it finds a home in the alternative worship scene. Like many others, I signed up for a service that aimed to bring club culture into contact with Christianity. The lights, visuals, tunes, atmosphere, content, and timing were all geared toward those who we thought were uncomfortable in church. And to some extent it worked, although it probably had more impact on the Christians that came along for the freedom than the non-Christians who turned up out of curiosity.

Other services and meetings have taken off and done wonders for plenty of people. The idea of bringing in sounds and images, reclaiming them from the world at large, and using them as touchstones, points of reference to which people can relate, has been one of the strengths of the scene. The same can be said for the way many people have grasped hold of contemporary theories on learning techniques. Briefly, the idea goes that when looking at the way people learn, there are broad categories which emerge with people taking on board bits of each. A logical-mathematical learner might learn through problem solving and challenges, while a verbal-linguistic learner might grasp things by reading, writing, and speaking about them. Visual-spatial learners are sparked by mental imagery while musical-rhythmic learners will find things fall into place when sound and rhythm are employed. Finally those termed bodily-kinesthetic learners will understand concepts and information best when they are accompanied by touch and movement. Too often the church environment, like secondary schools, caters to those who respond best to the spoken word, but with its open approach and light grasp of tradition, the alternative worship scene has helped to change that.

Yet, there are problems within the scene that need to be addressed. With so much attention being paid to the way things look, feel, smell, and so on, we can put too much emphasis on the way people respond. Services can get judged as successes or failures depending on the way people feel, which can all seem just a bit too self-indulgent. Yes, church meetings are about getting together and hanging out, but they are primarily there to help us praise God, learn more about Him, and tool up for extending the kingdom of God. It's good to enjoy them, but to bend them too much around our own appetites takes them dangerously close toward the view of God as hard-working entertainer and us as hard-to-please punters. Ironically, the alternative worship scene may also end up in much the same trap as the hardcore charismatic evangelicals from whom many recoil in the first place. In the extremes of both, there is a danger that complexity of thought comes a very distant second to a good old dose of gooey feelings.

It can also see us falling into the old New Labor trap: form over content. Instead of working on the message at the heart, we prefer to make sure it all looks nice and attractive. Unfortunately, it may be fun for the spin doctors, but it fails to fool most people in the long run. Christianity is not first and foremost an art movement, design school, or club for disgruntled performers. It is as the bride of Christ that we exist, His partner, here to team up with the work. Part of that does include celebrating God's creativity and diversity, but there's far more to it: discipling, teaching, healing, proclaiming, speaking, weeping, rejoicing, going, accepting, explaining. When we reduce Christianity to looking fluffy, we do God wrong.

It is important to face up to the facts that Paul highlighted to the Church at Colosse: Others may have thought that following the right rituals made you a better person, but Christianity breaks free from those restrictions. What are we committed to, the ritual or the relationship? Is the event the thing or is it the lifestyle which comes out of it that we are trying to work on?

Before we get too bogged down by church theory, let's move on to look at the less formal ways to bridge the gap between Church and culture. Much of it happens through individuals, and recent years have seen the rise of trendy Christians in all their bleached, pierced, and phat glory. Of all the cultural tribes and sub-groups around, the one that seems to have made the biggest impact—certainly as far as I can tell from the church culture I see—is skate culture. Talking to a friend last night I happened to mention the word "skatewear," and he looked blank. "What," he said, "like high-waisted, flared trousers and flouncy shirts?" A young Christian these days would be far less likely to confuse the world of the skateboard with that of the ice rink, but beyond the walls of the church, for people like my friend, it is a pretty unremarkable scene.

But the skate scene has taken off big-time in our little world, perhaps closely followed by the Ali G wannabe brigade. The skate look is comparatively easy to adopt, particularly for the middle-class Christian with a little cash to spend. Get the right brand of trainers, the right logo on your top, the right width of trousers and the right brand of pants peeping up over your trousers, top it off with something spiky, and you're well away. That the real skate scene is far less formulaic doesn't seem to matter to us, but I'll say no more about that for fear of coming off all cooler-than-thou about the whole thing.

We Christians love all that Generation X/Slacker stuff, and just the briefest look for Genesis X on the 'Net will turn up more sites written by Christians than you might have thought possible. The Genesis X/skate image sums up the way we'd like to be seen: cool, aware, relevant, and unafraid to rebel, if only just a little. But fashion is funny, whichever way you look at it. It's all tribal, and we all use clothes to express who we want people to take us for no matter how bizarre or conservative our tastes. In that sense there's nothing wrong with the Trendy Christian; it really makes little difference whether we're telling people, "Hey, I know about fashion, just look at my trainers" or "Hey, I know about fashion, just look at my Oxford brogues." It's all relative and probably shouldn't be taken that seriously.

Yet something inside feels as though this is a cop-out. The plain fact is that there is a certain degree of toe-treading that fashion does which doesn't sit comfortably with Christianity. Take the link between fashion and injustice. The pressures of consumerism have led to wide-scale oppression of workers throughout the developing world. While the trainers may be a ticket to fashion success, they can also be a tool of ungodly oppression. Isn't that one of the things that riled God about Israel, the people who "trample on the heads of the poor" (Amos 2:7)?

Or there's the link between fashion and a wandering away from God's view of His children. When we buy into the line that looking our best is important, it can only be a short step to believing that it is only when we look our best that we are truly loved. Carrying a little extra weight? Sorry, honey, you'll never be happy. Unable to afford the right label? Tough luck, your cool rating just took a dip. Whichever way you look at it, this line of thinking is totally in opposition to God's way of doing things. With both of these issues, sadly the Trendy Christian can do no more than bring the nice-looking bits of culture into the Church. Yes, it's nice to feel nice, but how sad a state is it when God's Word is infected with the dark heart of conditional self-worth and mindless materialism? Those are two flavors that most certainly have no place in the faith, but the damage is kicking in already. When church becomes a fashion show, when looking in the mirror comes in front of the Sunday morning ritual of looking for the Bible, church itself gets affected. All across the country, there are people leaving church because they find it dull and irrelevant, but there are also people turning their backs because they find it vacuous, pretentious, and unaccepting.

Finally, like it or not, most people aren't cool. The majority of the population shop in the most popular shops, wear the most popular clothes, and like the most popular music, which is why we're called the majority. If we're trying hard to make the Church as chic as we possibly can, then a simple question has to be asked: Why? It may make us feel good to be part of something cool, but our transparency will ultimately trip us up as we manage to only relate to a minority who are used to the passing of taste as often as the changing of socks. Christianity is for all. Yep, even the ones who don't look right.

Perhaps this Trendy Christian thing went right over your head, but maybe the core is relevant to more than just the phat ones: We need to watch out for the desire to bend too much in an effort to be relevant. OK, so we may be doing it out of the best of intentions, but the desire to make Christianity cool misses the point. Of course, it can be cool, vibrant, artistically challenging, and inspiring. But doing it just for those reasons is about as ridiculous a motive as they come.

Why Should We Even Bother Looking Out Anyway?

So why should we bother then? If all of the above is true, if our desire to look beyond the Church seems to result in at best foolishness and at worst hypocrisy, then why do it? The fact is that we have a duty to go out and do all the stuff that Jesus told us to. That means praying, healing, teaching, showing, serving, feeding, telling, and all that. It's a duty that we cannot ignore, and without the ability to relate to those outside of the Church and the dialogue itself, without the understanding of the issues that affect people today and an attempt to meet those needs, then we fail to fulfill some of our most essential obligations.

Can't we just do it from the comfort of our own pew? Not according to any of the Bible. Take, for example, the Big Daddy of "GO," the Apostle Paul. He was so fired up about sharing the message of the cross with people that he would do whatever he considered necessary to make it easier for people to hear and understand. Poor old Timothy found this out at great personal pain when he and Paul first met. Because Paul thought that he would get a better reception from the Jews in the area, Paul had Timothy circumcised. Yet in his later letters he seems to contradict himself:

"Circumcision is nothing and uncircumcision is nothing. Keeping God's commands is what counts" (1 Cor. 7:19).

"For in Christ Jesus neither circumcision nor uncircumcision has any value. The only thing that counts is faith expressing itself through love" (Gal. 5:6).

"Neither circumcision nor uncircumcision means anything; what counts is a new creation" (Gal. 6:15).

Hardly the words of a man who would do the deed on a young lad he had barely met before. But this is Paul through and through: desperate to do whatever he could to spread the news. Likewise, he was supremely aware of the liberty at the heart of Christianity, but he also was able to keep others in mind. If his actions were going to offend, he'd put his own feelings second, as he makes clear here:

> But food does not bring us near to God; we are no worse
> if we do not eat, and no better if we do. Be careful, how-
> ever, that the exercise of your freedom does not become
> a stumbling block to the weak. For if anyone with a

weak conscience sees you who have this knowledge eating in an idol's temple, won't he be emboldened to eat what has been sacrificed to idols? So this weak brother, for whom Christ died, is destroyed by your knowledge. When you sin against your brothers in this way and wound their weak conscience, you sin against Christ. Therefore, if what I eat causes my brother to fall into sin, I will never eat meat again, so that I will not cause him to fall. (1 Cor. 8:8-13)

Why should we engage? Not only because we can, but because we must. After all, isn't that what God did?

Does Everything Have to Be Brought in to Be Redeemed?

In Jeremiah we read about the Israelites who had been carried off into exile by Nebuchadnezzar. Living in Babylon, a long way from home, it's tempting to imagine that they felt as though all was at a loss. It's true—things were pretty bad, but God's perspective opened their eyes to a glorious reality. Through the prophet Jeremiah they received a command to "build houses and settle down; plant gardens and eat what they produce" (Jer. 29:5). They might have been in exile, oppressed, and in a foreign land, but they were told to settle and make roots.

God's plans are more than capable of being carried out in situations that we might consider to be less than ideal. This is something that we appear to have missed, as there is a strong tendency within the Church to believe that for something to be of worth to God, it has to be brought into the Church. It happens when people become Christians and they start to believe that instead of being a regular plumber, musician, administrator, or whatever they were before, they need to be a Christian plumber, musician, engineer, or whatever. And how do we tell them to do this? Come and plumb Christians' drains, come and play in the church, come and work in the church office.

How far removed is this from a Hebrew position that saw worth in all work? Why did they go for that line? Because God created the world, not just believers, altars, and sacrificial animals. God stepped up as author of all our talents, and despite the fact that it makes things so much neater if we do, we cannot select which ones have talents that are godly and which ones do not. Of course, we all have the potential for being used in ungodly ways, from the power of music to the art of communication, but we must learn to see the worth in the exercise of all talents. If not, we create an image of God that depicts Him as blowing hot and cold toward humanity. Was God not bothered about Jesus being a carpenter? Was it, "Yeah, yeah, nice, but can't you just get ON with it?"

Gifts are to be used for God's glory, and not just in church. Is a cut flower more beautiful when it stands in church than when it grows in the field? Of course not, so why do we persist in viewing the Church as the only forum in which God takes pleasure? The facts of the incarnation show the truth of the matter: that God chose physical form to save the world.

What Does the World Look Like with Glasses?

Remember the deal with having short- or long-sighted views of how God works? Remember how we can be tempted to view the world solely as troubling and repulsive or appealing and alluring? Well, these are lessons we all need to return to. Unlike school examinations, it is not a case of completing the task and checking it off as dealt with, never to be returned to again. Gaining a view of the world that is in line with God's idea of focus is a constant and ever-evolving process. Perhaps there are three areas in which we can expect to work: seeing the world as a place created by God, as a place in which we are prepared to be used by God, and as a place through which we are prepared to receive from God. Life outside of church is not the same as that which goes on beneath the belltower; there are differences between the two. How should we react to it? Here's what Paul suggests: "For everything God created is good, and nothing is to be rejected if it is received with thanksgiving" (1 Tim. 4:4).

Dynamic, authentic, and godly—that's how the Church should look with the proper view of culture in place. Why not work on creating such a view ourselves, both within ourselves and the Church at large? Perhaps then we will begin to understand that viewing the world is a question of conduit rather than source, that it's about seeing God as speaking through other things rather than declaring the other things as the source of God.

"Jesus made His business the
inclusion of all, from the winners
to the losers."

6

What Do We Look Like Together?

What Happens When We Bring Others In?

Can we be honest here? Are we really that welcoming of outsiders in the Church? I mean, we hardly make things easy for others to join us, do we? When the invitation for them to come and stand with us side by side in front of the mirror gets taken up, all too often we get a little stressed out. It's all that close-up stuff that troubles us, you see, the fact that so many people join the Church without the protective clothing that takes us months to put on. There they are, odd and vulnerable, showing off their scars and wounds to a watching church, not looking an awful lot like the rest of us. And if we're honest, we get a little embarrassed at the sight of it all. The fact is that we have become so used to the assumption that to be a good Christian is to want a six-pack, wear the mask, ditch the glasses, and all that, that we find it hard when we meet Christians for whom those traits mean nothing at all. Of course, within a few weeks, the fresh Christian will have thankfully started to look a little more normal, which is a tremendous relief to the rest of us, but every once in a while there's a headstrong one who simply refuses to conform. No matter how many times we tell him that he just needs to "let go and let God," he remains stubbornly resolute. How rude is that?

I've got a friend who is precisely one of these people. She's received more tellings-off (sorry, I mean quiet words of encouragement from the Lord) than most people I know, and all because she doesn't fit into the narrow model that some around her believe to be the True Christian. She's no rebel, and she's still hanging in there with church, looking for a place to call home, which, all things considering, shows plenty of character. But somehow she just seems to attract grief, and as her career requires a lot of relocating, she's been to a few churches in her time and experienced more than the odd cold shoulder. Like the first time she went out on a "social" with a new church. She met up with them at the pub, and while most of the church crowd there were strangers to her, she got chatting with a couple of them who seemed nice enough. Nice enough, that is until she stopped asking them about their own lives and answered a question about the sort of thing she likes to do with her spare time. Telling them that she liked clubbing was a mistake. Did she not know that such places were wrong, that they were evil? How could she call herself a Christian and behave so? The conversation didn't get much better with the others, and she spent the rest of the evening putting up with the accusatory stares from the church crowd as she chatted to a group of people who had nothing to do with church and just happened to be there for a few beers after work.

This experience added nicely to her sense of surprise when, some time later, she moved cities and visited another new church. "Hello," said a friendly chap who she had seen passing around the collection plate. "And what do you do?" She told him that she was a psychologist. He told her that she wasn't a Christian. "The Lord is the only true healer," he huffed before walking away to welcome someone else.

Then there was the church that she went to for a couple of years. Looking back now, her reflections reveal a sad truth that we find hard to accept. "When I started going, I felt good about myself, who I was, and how I looked. But over the months the pressure to look your best, to wear the latest clothes, and to have the thinnest arms just got to me. It was all very competitive but totally unspoken. I ended up feeling second rate and unhappy, that God preferred those who looked the best."

She's not alone, and the well-publicized decline in church attendance tells us as much. Even in the pockets where church appears to be growing, there is a sense that unless you fit snugly in with the ideals, attitudes, and aspirations, you'll have a rough ride in the church. And do you know the saddest thing about it all? It's been happening for years. Ever since Emperor Constantine converted to Christianity and made it the state religion in 324 A.D., our faith has felt the subtle pressure of change. Where the early Christians were persecuted, Constantine made them safe. Where the life of the Church had previously been expressed through a variety of actions, it became a series of meetings. Where Christianity had been a risk, it became a tool for social acceptance. Perhaps even today, in spite of all the empty buildings and declining attendance, we find it hard to shrug off almost 1,700 years of believing that it is up to people to fit into the church. Perhaps things are coming full circle as we return to a time when it is up to the Church to work hard at fitting around the people.

But isn't this all a bit much? In reality, the Church is full of people who seem happy enough to be there, so can fitting in really be such an important issue? A decent enough point if it weren't for the fact that those who find it hard to fit in are conspicuous by their absence. While many people find that church suits them down to the ground, others find themselves having to bend and modify in order to conform. For those who cannot do the first and won't do the second, there's not much of a choice left: Exist as a pariah on the furthest outreaches of church, or pack up and leave. Most do just that, and we hear nothing more from them. Could this be pure fantasy? If only it were. There are more people "out there" who have a tale to tell about a personal experience of church than many "in here" would like to believe. When I think about my friends who have nothing to do with church, the majority of them have had some brush with church at some point in their life. Sadly, for most of them that past experience doesn't rank as one of their best. If your personal experience doesn't confirm it, then the statistics do just as well. According to church research, and published in *The Tide Is Running Out* by Dr. Peter Brierley, Sunday church attendance has declined by an average of 2,200 people every week in the 1990s. That means an awful lot of growth in the numbers of ex-churchgoers out there.

What Makes It Hard to Fit In?

It's a tough old thing to face up to, but for plenty of people church leaves them cold. They may have had wild experiences of God in the past, they may even have been fired up and feisty with the best of them, but get them to cast their mind back, and for some the whole deal is about as important to them as the color of their school uniform. And, of course, it's not just church that gets put in that "whatever" box, but God too. And that, to say the least, is a shame.

For others, church has inflicted wounds that remain tender to the touch for years to come. Whether it was the pain of being left unnoticed on the outskirts or the hurt of a direct attack, there are plenty walking around with a story to tell. Again, this is not the way that it's supposed be. Is it? Of course, sometimes things are difficult: personalities clash, people can be awkward, disruptive, and downright infuriating. Stretched, pressured, and ill-equipped as the Church can be, chasing after these difficulties with a tricky individual can come second to making sure that the rest of the flock are safe and secure. But how sad is that if we're losing people because of logistics? If it's more staff we need, then perhaps it's time to start selling off a little of the family silver to expand the staff team. I'm sure there's room for the extra souls in heaven, and they'd look so much nicer than snapshots of land, art, and fine buildings.

A Different View

Whether it's about culture or evangelism, friendship or ambition, the simple fact that a church member possesses a view that deviates from the party line may be enough to make the waters choppy. This is all tied in with the cult of the six-pack and the sweet tooth the Church can have for all things dualistic. There's a strong flavor of "separate is best" running throughout, but we've been through this already. What turns the presence of difference of opinion into tension can be found in our approach to the way church is run. Our meetings give little space for dialogue, choosing instead to push out the unspoken message that we, the congregation, are there to sit quietly and attentively during the talks. The knowledge is there to be imparted to us, and ours is not the job to question, just to accept. The fact that this approach has long been rejected by the education system doesn't seem to bother us, and we carry on regardless with the preachers preaching and the congregation soaking it up. It's true that midweek meetings in smaller settings offer a better chance for people to question and discuss issues, but by relegating dialogue to these meetings, the unspoken message is as strong as ever: Leave your questions at the door when you turn up on Sunday.

Many of us can't help but ask questions, but too often the act of questioning gets labeled as doubt and a wholesale lack of faith. We should all be working hard at testing this faith for ourselves. Christianity is more than capable of standing up to it, and in the same way that Jesus didn't leave the questioning of Peter at "Who do people say I am?" we need to be working out our response to the question "Who do you say I am?" This is what got Paul so hot under the collar, the fact that the Christian is not justified by deeds but by faith. Put it another way, and we conclude that we're not here to learn how to do a decent impression of a Christian, but to live the life for ourselves. It's not about mumbled responses and well-performed rituals; it's about personal relationship with the risen Jesus.

The Prodigal Problems

Leaving church was a hard thing to do, and during my time away I struggled to work out just what camp I fell into. Was I an angry young man, raging at the injustices thrown at me by a rotten system, or did I simply not care, writing the whole package off as an irrelevant part of my past? It was only in leaving that I finally started to probe and dissect my beliefs, and over time the questions kept coming. If I'd assumed that they would stop when I came back, I was wrong. That was when things really got confusing. It may have been a return to the faith of a few years before, but it looked completely different. Just how much of those old beliefs would I keep around me?

My old black-and-white view of things failed to have quite the spiritual zing that once had be captivated. Previously, the good versus bad logic that underpinned my approach to church versus the world felt like the only way forward. Yet somehow, I knew that I had matured, that my years away were not wasted. I felt that I had more to bring to my beliefs, that I was a stronger Christian because of my recent experiences. But did this sit well with the old way of viewing things? It did not and threw me between the extremes of small-minded paranoia and free-flowing DIY spirituality like a particularly unfortunate ice hockey puck. One minute I'd be ranting, the next I'd be dribbling. Not a pretty sight at all, but while these swings were frustrating, the real problem lay at the heart. At times I felt alienated by my own beliefs, and it was only through the help of sound, level-headed Christians that I began to see the light.

The old idea of gifts needing to be brought in and used in a church setting caused trouble too, as the pressure to show spiritual commitment through church overtime helped reinforce the beliefs that did me no good. Where I was looking for a faith that helped me survive right where I was, I ended up with time pressures that made it almost impossible not to withdraw. Frustrations soon followed, and there were many times when I kicked back against what I felt was a system that was failing to practice what it supposedly preached.

Finally, there was a large dose of embarrassment over my previous behavior. Not so much the years spent a-wandering, but the period before that when all I wanted was a warm fuzz and a couple of shaking spasms to round the evening service off nicely. Much of it had come to a head halfway through my "time off" when a school friend's death made me stop and think. A few months after he died, I wrote (and you'll have to forgive the whiffy title I gave it):

The Trouble with Church

All that emphasis on movement of the Holy Spirit, it just

left me conscious of whether or not I was being touched. I needed to show that I was being touched too and used to feel like it was important to exhibit the correct emotions. Today I still feel that way, the need to act the right part. After John died, I tried to make myself cry. I couldn't. But I felt like I should cry. My head just felt too full, as if I was watching myself move, act and be, working out how I was doing, how well I was scoring at playing the griever. I kept pressing the button marked "CRY" but nothing happened. Nothing ever happened.

Back at church some years later, I found myself totally wary of showing "too much" emotion. There was an added element of confusion as many of the feelings I was experiencing at church reminded me tingle for tingle of the ones I'd had on Ecstasy in the past. The pressure would come back into my head twice as strong, and a running commentary would start up: "You're feeling lightheaded—is that good? Is that real? Are you faking it? What happens next? What would happen if I started to fall over? Am I starting to fall over? What about if ... ?" On and on it would go. All that advice about "letting go and letting God" didn't help much either, as pretty soon I'd decided that I was better off ditching the feelings side of faith altogether.

Too specific perhaps, only relevant to myself? I'm not so sure. For many people who've come through experiences of Ecstasy, the perspective on intense feelings is bound to be different. But the solution is not to be found in blanking off all feelings, of throwing the baby out with the bath water. Jesus' parable of the son who squandered his inheritance and returned to find the arms of his father wide open leaves it up to us to imagine what happens after the celebration of his return has finished. Consequences are a fact of life, and living with them involves facing them head-on and being prepared to learn from them, changing as necessary. Surely God is able to cope with a wayward past? I guess the real question is: Are His people able to?

The Uncomfortable Pews

On a weekend away a friend of mine was chatting with a whole bunch of people that she only knew on a fairly superficial level. They all studied together, but nothing beyond the bare facts of life and opinions on sandwich fillings had ever passed between them. Then something happened. While they were away on a study weekend for their course, a workshop vaguely brought up the subject of spirituality. It was the briefest of mentions, but somehow it caught the imagination, and later that night as they sat around having a drink and a chat, the subject came back. One by one the people started telling their own stories.

There was a girl who had felt the lowest in her life. Her father had died; her boyfriend left; and her life was in a mess. Church had never figured in her life before, so she was surprised when she felt the urge to go along to a service one Sunday. She'd passed the church loads of times before; it had been as much a part of the landscape as the park and shops around the corner. She didn't know what to expect as she went in, but sitting at the back seemed like the right thing to do. The service came and went, and all she did was cry. The tears came through the songs and the prayers, the sermon and even the odd bit at the end where people went up to the front and talked quietly in twos and threes. She went home feeling better.

The next week she went back. There were more tears on the back row, more tears that she didn't understand. Again she felt better for going, but still had no idea what it was that drew her there. "I think it was something to do with the fact that I had space to think about nothing," she said.

Weeks came and went, still with her taking her seat in silence on Sunday mornings. These days she went prepared, pockets full of neatly folded tissues on the way there, bulging with soggy ones on the way back. But one day, she turned up, and the tears never came. She never went back. "In the nine weeks I went," she told the group, "no one ever spoke to me."

There was an older guy who had been going to church for years. He grew up there and laughed as he could remember all the old choruses he used to sing, ones like "Joy Is the Flag" and "You Shall Go Out with Joy." They seemed strange now, as it had been years since he had been inside a church. As he grew up, he spent more and more time there, eventually taking a job working for the local bishop. He was happy there, finding the job stimulating, challenging, and exciting. He was married too, and talked about getting ordained. Then he started to question his sexuality. Nothing major, just queries, wonders, the sort of things that he wanted to talk over with someone who he trusted, someone who could help him make sense of it all. So he talked to his boss, the bishop. "This cannot happen," he was told. "You cannot have these thoughts and remain in the church." End of story. No more conversation. Within months he had been frozen out of his job, pushed out to the fringes of church. His marriage failed, and he eventually started a new life living with a guy. "I don't know what I believe now," he told people. "I don't feel as if I ever left the church. It feels more like they rejected me. I'm still looking for God, I suppose, and nothing I've found has got me closer to Him than Christianity. I just don't think they'd ever really want me."

My friend spent the evening in tears as person after person told of moments when they'd reached out to the Church but found nothing but rules and cozy insularity blocking their way. Others had been pushed away even before they'd got to the church doors, and one had even been told that the police would be called if she didn't stop making a nuisance of herself. She was only changing a punctured tire on her car outside the entrance. If we really want to know how comfortable and welcoming we are, how good we are at accepting strangers and giving them all they need and more, then let's not ask the people who are on the inside; let's not just look at the success stories. Being real means facing up to the harsh, ugly truth, unpleasant as it is. Sometimes we just can't be bothered. Sometimes people are too much hard work, too much hassle, too far away from the soft targets than we'd like them to be. Sometimes we just prefer it the way it is.

The Problem with Failure

A new assistant pastor got up to deliver his first sermon at church. We'd been going for a couple of years, and there were no more than sixty of us at the meeting. Even that felt like far too many though, as he kicked off his debut talk with a line that had me bent double with wincing anxiety. "I haven't read my Bible for three weeks." *No! Somebody stop him!* Furtive eyes glanced around the room. Others had noticed. *Should we jump him now before he makes an even bigger spectacle? What about if he starts talking about his personal sin? Is there any way that we can hypnotize the congregation afterward and make them forget so horrific a line?*

It was all rank hypocrisy, of course. I'd hardly picked up my Bible since the previous summer when it had spent a week wedged behind a shaky sink and become moldy with the damp. As it had dried out, all the pages had stuck together, providing me with a painful reminder for years to come of just how little of the Bible I'd actually read since then. I eventually bought a new one eighteen months later when a friend I had explained the story to in private brought it up at a Bible study. Every passage he told us to turn to was accompanied by a face-reddening rip as I pried open yet another buried treasure. I could handle Malachi and Philemon, but had I really read nothing from Matthew, Mark, Luke, John, and Acts in all that time?

I digress. The fact is that the new pastor's confession just wasn't the sort of thing that ought to have been broadcast from the front. It was an admission of failure, a serious black mark against the guy's name, and completely at odds with the tide of church culture that hopes to keep failure at bay. That's right, we can't stand it, and the merest whiff of imperfection—unless it's surrounded by some tales of serious spiritual success—is enough to raise more than the odd eyebrow.

A friend found this out to his cost some years ago. He'd grown up in a Christian home—his dad a pastor—and had settled down in a new town in his early twenties and got stuck into a vibey church. It was the kind of church that put a lot of value on the family, and it did wonders with those who had young kids. So there was a culture, an expectation that people would settle down and marry young. This suited my friend, who hooked with a good church girl. Everyone said they were great together, and pretty soon they were engaged and then married. Big celebration, lots of happiness, plenty of pats on the back, and warm hugs from the church.

Then it went wrong. They got on their honeymoon, and it all changed. She'd kept things from him throughout their engagement, mainly the fact that she was on medication to help manage depression. Now that they were married, she was a different person, as if she had given up trying to appear "normal" and was showing him her true colors. Things went from bad to worse, and within weeks of arriving back at home he would sometimes have to lock himself away in the bedroom to stay safe during her low periods. Within months he knew the marriage was over—it had never really begun. They both knew what needed to happen, and they started divorce proceedings.

When the church found out, they reacted badly. Had things really gotten so bad that it had come to this? What about prayer and marriage counseling—had they not tried it? But this was way beyond marriage counseling, and brows furrowed in sympathy. This was a question of serious mental illness, and both needed to get out; she to get help, and he to recover from the stress. Divorce was the best solution, and as they both agreed it was for the best, it would be quick and as painless as divorce can be. This was not good enough for the church. Divorce looked bad, was against God's plan, and should be avoided. They applied pressure on him to stop the proceedings and go instead for an annulment, to have the marriage declared invalid on the grounds that he had been tricked. This would have meant court appearances, evidence, and hearings. Doctors would have been dragged in, and she would have had to face solicitors out to paint her in the worst light possible. Where was the sense, compassion, and love in that, asked my friend. But he only ever got the same answer: It was better than divorce. Eventually he left the church.

We have a problem with what we perceive as failure. Too often we can feel guilty if we allow the merest stain of failure to darken our pure white robes of faith. Letting a non-Christian in on the fact that our life might not be a bed of roses, admitting to the realities of the struggle, owning up to doubt, fear, and confusion, they all can leave us with a hangover that tells us we have done wrong. Can that really be right?

The Church's reaction to "mistakes" can at times almost be automatic. Of course, we should be presenting God in the best light, so the logic might go. Why on earth would we ever do anything to discourage people? Sadly, we come up with our own conclusions and sense of discouragement when we realize that our lives just don't match up to the ideal placed before us.

It's not all fertilizer for despair, though. There are plenty of people around who use the platform to show their weaknesses, to be honest with others, to show themselves for who they really are. This is a brave position to take, and all who do it need plenty of support and encouragement.

Why?

But why have we ended up here? What has gone on to make us so scared of failure? Perhaps the answer is as simple, frustrating, and vaguely familiar as this: We've forgotten whose battle we're fighting. At the risk of boring you with it again, remember the deal with Joshua and the mystery swordsman? It's God's battle, not ours. Christianity is about the army, not the individual. If one person trips up, then viewed in isolation it could be seen as bad news. But if the person trips up and those around him learn more about their own path, if they can help their partner up and become better united through it, then it really isn't so bad after all. We might all want to be the hero, to believe that our successes or failings are absolutely vital to the Christian cause, but in reality we're all way down the ranking system. Foot soldiers, if you like. I'm going to start talking ants and colonies and the collective soon, so let's just leave it here, shall we? Our failings are not the last word. Not only are we in this together, but the burden of victory does not rest with us anyway. That's God's bag.

How Does God Feel About 'Failure'?

First up let's ditch the term "failure." It's too harsh, too final for what we're talking about. Instead, we'll refer to them as mistakes, and we'll see that they aren't exactly rare in the Bible. Take Samson, for example. Set apart for God by his parents from his very first moments, Samson's life was seriously special. While most people took a Nazarite vow for a certain period of time—no razors, wine, or dead animals—Samson was going to be doing it his whole life. And whether it was solely because of this that God blessed him, we may never know, but bless him He did. Just check out the power here:

> Samson went down to Timnah together with his father and mother. As they approached the vineyards of Timnah, suddenly a young lion came roaring toward him. The Spirit of the Lord came upon him in power so that he tore the lion apart with his bare hands as he might have torn a young goat. But he told neither his father nor his mother what he had done. (Judg. 14:5-6)

That's some power he's got, ripping apart a lion with his bare hands. But as we see a couple of verses later, he's not all squeaky clean. He has already forced his parents to allow him to marry a girl from the foreign but nearby town of Timnah, and one day: "Some time later, when he went back to marry her, he turned aside to look at the lion's carcass. In it was a swarm of bees and some honey, which he scooped out with his hands and ate as he went along. When he rejoined his parents, he gave them some, and they too ate it. But he did not tell them that he had taken the honey from the lion's carcass" (Judg. 14:8-9).

For a guy who is not supposed to be touching anything to do with alcohol, what is he doing in a vineyard? Come to think of it, why is he prodding about inside a dead lion if he's not supposed to touch dead animals? Samson's inability to put God before his own desires—whether curiosity, lust, or arrogance—gets him in trouble continually. This revisiting of the scene where God performed a miracle is symptomatic of Samson's approach. The good gets used for bad, and holy gets tainted. But God stays with him.

He can't leave the lion alone even when he's about to get married, and he poses a riddle to the groomsmen: "Out of the eater, something to eat; out of the strong, something sweet" (Judg. 14:14). The riddle gets used to make Samson potentially very rich, with each man standing to lose a "linen garment" if he fails to get it. These were serious threads, and a grown man might expect to only own one set in his entire life. Samson, schmuck that he is, says that he'll hand out thirty if they solve the riddle.

The long and the short of it is that they do solve the riddle, and Samson is in trouble. You'd think that God would be washing His hands of the man by now, but something else happens: "Then the Spirit of the Lord came upon him in power. He went down to Ashkelon, struck down thirty of their men, stripped them of their belongings and gave their clothes to those who had explained the riddle. Burning with anger, he went up to his father's house. And Samson's wife was given to the friend who had attended him at his wedding" (Judg. 14:19-20).

This is perhaps a little too much to handle. God allows him to make a thirty-mile hike to a coastal town and then helps him murder and rob his way out of the debt. Why? What possible explanation can be given for this outrageous behavior?

The pattern carries on, but not before Samson does what he is there for and begins "the deliverance of Israel from the hands of the Philistines" (Judg. 13:5). There's the famous story of him with Delilah, where again he plays games with the blessings God has given him. But apart from the fulfilment of the prophecy about beginning the deliverance, there is only one other decent clue that might help us in our quest for an answer to the question of why.

> Now the temple was crowded with men and women; all the rulers of the Philistines were there, and on the roof were about three thousand men and women watching Samson perform. Then Samson prayed to the Lord, "O Sovereign Lord, remember me. O God, please strengthen me just once more, and let me with one blow get revenge on the Philistines for my two eyes." Then Samson reached toward the two central pillars on which the temple stood. Bracing himself against them, his right hand on the one and his left hand on the other, Samson said, "Let me die with the Philistines!" Then he pushed with all his might, and down came the temple on the rulers and all the people in it. Thus he killed many more when he died than while he lived. (Judg. 16:27-31)

Killing the Philistines was another step along the way to fulfilling the prophecy over his life. While I don't want to go down the predestination/we-are-all-God's-puppets route, it does seem that viewed from a distance, Samson's life—despite the fact that he failed to fulfil his potential as he was so busy thinking with his pants—was used by God. God used Samson despite his sin. For a God who is ultimately bigger than sin itself, I suppose it kind of makes sense that He can use us despite our sin. What is truly amazing, though, is the fact that He does use us despite our sin.

Our failings (sorry, wrong word) are not the end of the story. Our lives themselves are not the end of the story. We are part of a continuum, God's ever-evolving kingdom. To believe that our mistakes have no place is to try and contort and twist ourselves into a shape that simply cannot be held. To believe this type of thing is to puff ourselves up, to inflate our egos and say, "I am so important, my personal success is so essential that I CANNOT FAIL. If I do, then life as we know may well CEASE." We lose sight of the fact that—as we've said before—God works through the individual for the universal. And that simply won't do.

How Did Jesus Do It?

So let's bring it back to Jesus, shall we? While mistakes, failings, sins were not on His resume, the very heart of His work on earth sheds light on the whole issue of belonging. He was far more concerned about the salvation of the individual than perhaps we give Him credit for, as His parable bonanza in Luke 15 makes clear. There's the story of the shepherd who leaves the flock safely penned in to go out and find the stray sheep, a celebration of uniqueness and individuality if ever there was one; and it contrasts the love of God nicely with the exclusiveness of the Pharisees. Even the title underlines the truth, focusing in on the lost sheep rather than the found flock.

Or there's the one about the lost coin: widow loses coin, widow finds coin. But why would she bother looking for a worthless coin? It was perhaps part of a ceremonial headdress and boosted the self-esteem of one who would have been on the margins without a husband.

Then there's the story about the lost sons. One goes off to blow his inheritance while the other stays at home and thinks he has to work to earn his father's affection. It is the father who plays the central role, pulling in both lads from the extremes, but allowing them to wander. The truth of their belonging cannot be better summed up than in the image of the old man hitching up his robes and sprinting out to greet his wandering son. How ridiculous, unnecessary, and undignified. How very God.

Individuals, individuals, individuals. The mantra is worth remembering: People are of worth. God values them, chases them, lavishes affection on them, welcomes them, treasures them, forgives them, and loves them. Scoot back a few pages though, and you'll see some text about how this whole thing's a team activity, that the battle is God's not ours. And this is the mad paradox at the heart of it all: Jesus lavished all He had, gave up His life for you, for me, and at the same time we're not the top of the bill. Unique, yet one of billions is a weird tension that we all have to live with, but both are eternal truths that remain active in our own lives. Jesus taught the lesson well through His life, and it makes sense that we should do all we can to make sure that the bride is in step with the groom. If Jesus explains the reason why He eats with sinners this way, if this is His "I'll tell you why I go out of my way to make the wrong people feel welcome," then this should be our mission statement, too.

Jesus made His business the inclusion of all, from the winners to the losers. It's true that He saved His harshest words for those who considered themselves the religious success stories of the day, while His most reckless and lavish acts were poured out on those who many would have thought were "poor in spirit." How great a battle plan is that? He got under the skin of complacency, surprised the pants off dejection, and offered salvation to all, regardless of background. Are we really following His lead?

"The aim is not our own satisfaction,
but the strengthening of the Church."

7

Why Am I Looking in This Mirror Anyway?

Help! I'm an Airhead Christian

I mean, just what is the point of all this mirror stuff? All this talk about getting a better focus on the world, about learning to show a more honest face to others as well as understanding more of God's take on things; well, isn't it all just a bit self-indulgent? Isn't it just another case of Christians talking about nothing other than themselves? Haven't we spent enough time in front of the mirror yet? Of course, it's right to wonder exactly what all this is for; if it's introspection for introspection's sake, then there's little point in it all. But hopefully these gazing sessions will give us something to work on, something to mold what stares back at us into a better form. But even though I reckon that life without spiritual six-packs, stagnant water, masks, sneers, tears, poor eyesight, and an uncomfortable pew is possible, I can't help thinking that it all feels a bit too much like hard work.

And this whole process of asking questions and searching for answers really is at odds with the way that I've felt at different points in my life. There have been occasions where the mere mention of doing anything that remotely resembled thought when it came to sussing out my faith would have had me doubled over in shame-faced agony. Question why I do things? You must be joking. Wonder about the possibility that I might have got things wrong? Leave it out, sunshine.

But the truth is that even though it's never nice being confronted with the cold flannel of reality, be confronted we must. I have to admit that I've had my fair share of wake-ups over the years. There was the time I realized that wars were not fought for just one day in just one large field, with everyone going home at the end to put plasters on their grazed knees. Or the day it dawned on me that talking about drugs at length did not make me an interesting person. But there's one that sticks out more painfully than all the others, one that even rivals the day when I realized I was about to lose my left testicle. (Thankfully I didn't, but perhaps that's not quite the sort of Naked Christian you're interested in.) The revelation I have in mind is far more embarrassing even than that, and while at least it didn't cause me to walk like John Wayne for a month, the symptoms were plain for all to see. I'm talking about the time that I realized I was an Airhead Christian.

The Revelation

Things had been going so well, too. I'd been doing the old carpe diem thing at church, seizing the day, living life in the spiritual fast lane and all that. The prophecies had been flowing, the tongues were almost fluent, and I had the knack of making my left eyelid twitch on command, which came in mighty useful whenever I wanted to pretend that God wanted a quiet word in my ear. So things were good. Very good in fact, and I was enjoying church, God, and the whole thing more than ever.

And then I went on a French exchange. I don't know what got me down the most: the fact that out of the two hundred students to choose from, the teachers believed that Isabelle Thomasset and family were my absolute ideal match, or the fact that after two days *dans la maison Thomasset* I had been the subject of three separate formal complaints back to my school. For a good Christian lad, this was quite a shock, especially as the reasons given were the fact that I was a) mad, b) dangerous, and c) "making zuh family un'appy."

But I'm rambling. The point is that by the time the fourth day came around, I was feeling low. I'd exhausted every last ounce of tactical diplomacy and had taken to spending my days feeling miserable in cafés. When feeling miserable in cafés no longer made me feel nice and artsy, I settled down to some serious woe. For the rest of the fortnight things got worse with the family and worse with my soul. And where was God in all this? Good question, and one that I was asking on an almost hourly basis. How come I felt so low? How come He felt so far away? How come He wasn't answering my calls? The days passed, and I become increasingly desperate, finally giving God an ultimatum: if He didn't touch me right there, right then, if He didn't show me that He was there, that He was listening and that He cared, it was over. I meant it, too. The minutes went by, and nothing happened. Nothing but silence.

More silence.

That was it. I heard no word of encouragement from God. I felt no warm glow of His presence. I didn't shake, cry, or start to sing out loud. I just stayed there, feeling numb. I felt nothing, and in my misguided way, I assumed that this meant that God was off the map. I'd spent years walking along that path, assuming that Jesus was alive because I could feel His presence, and it was only now that I had cause to question it. All my years of refusing to question things for myself, to find out more about God than how He made me feel had left me high and dry. Instead of thought, reflection, questioning, I had lived my life by another compass altogether: feelings. Although I couldn't put a name to it then, it was at this point that I realized I'd been living life as an Airhead Christian. Sadly, I turned my back on God.

Telltale Signs

Perhaps I'll never be an ex-Airhead Christian. Instead I'm coming to terms with the fact that I will always be a recovering Airhead Christian, one whose symptoms are thankfully in remission. It's been years since I wandered back to my old ways, but you never count yourself free of something like that. I wonder if there's a therapy group I could go to? "My name is Craig, and I'm an ..."

So what about those symptoms? Airhead Christians come in a variety of shapes and sizes, and it strikes me that there were three main outworkings of the state that enveloped me for more than six years. First was, as mentioned already, a massive emphasis on feelings. These puppies were the judge and jury, and they took precedence over everything else, especially logical thought. They became my trusted guide as I judged whether something was of God by whether I felt "at peace" about it. If I didn't, then the plan went out the window—unless I felt particularly passionate, in which case I was OK to carry on. This came in particularly handy when faced with the extremes of my affections. If I was facing something that I really didn't want to do—inviting someone along to a meeting perhaps or going out of my way to be nice to a person I didn't like—then more often than not I'd feel annoyed or nervous rather than peaceful. Bingo, I was off the hook. Likewise if there was something that I had my eye on—like setting my ambitions on Christian Celebrity—the fact that I felt passionate about it was enough to convince me that God was 100 percent behind me. In this way, the feelings were used as a hearing aid for God's voice. A murmur of excitement meant God was happy while a pang of anxiety proved beyond any doubt that He was upset. It may have been simple, but I'm afraid it was both ineffective and misguided.

Then there was the shying away from knowledge. Theologians became the third most despised people in my universe (behind satanists and journalists) for the simple reason that they were diluting the power of God. Or so I thought. The way I saw it the pursuit of knowledge led to a stale and lifeless faith. Anyone who was obsessed with detail and historical fact had failed to understand the central message of the Bible: Jesus was alive and ready to party. These poor spiritual geeks would never amount to anything, and I was sure that they were the absolute spitting image of the New Testament Pharisees. As far as I was concerned, the scientists still had Jesus' blood on their hands, and they deserved to pay.

Finally, you could tell I was an Airhead Christian by the importance I placed on experiences. Wherever it was, whenever it was happening, if it was a big deal on the Christian scene, I wanted to be there. I was aiming at getting my spiritual passport as widely stamped as possible, and in my effort to be the king of "been there, done that," I attended plenty of conferences and meetings. If I couldn't be there in person, I'd get the tape, but I don't think I ever bothered with books. In fact, I only ever bought one Christian market book in this period. It was called *Happiness*, and I gave up after the first chapter as it quite obviously didn't work. Things were better live, but secondhand would do, and after one meeting with a visiting "prophet" that only the top brass of the church had gone to, word came back that a very special prophecy had been given out: "Revival will start twenty miles northwest of London." Standing in the pub looking at the map of the M25, a select few of us got steadily more excited as we realized that the coordinates matched our church precisely. The prospect of being so close to the action had me on a high for days, so much so that I thought I'd never come down, and prompted numerous entries into my notebook. Here's the best: "Give me the most mystical and powerful encounter with You that I've ever had. Jesus, I am sorry for not being hungry enough, but now I am. Please give me a really big one."

Oh dear.

Am I the Only One?

Despite the fact that the paranoid in me does wonder sometimes, the truth is that there are more of us Airhead Christians about the place than perhaps we'd like to believe. And while I'm glad for the company, I can't help feeling that we might do well to keep an eye out, all things considered. This re-jigging of the Christian's priorities, this preference for emotion over understanding, the easy ride over the uphill struggle does not go without consequences, and it is these consequences that show the extent to which the Church today has been molded. However subtle the lessons, it would seem that they have not gone unnoticed; the signs are everywhere.

No Way Through the Desert

We struggle with the difficult seasons of the Christian life. Why? Because we can end up having no frame of reference through which to view the desert experiences. While we might not be sure about when they will come (although if you're planning a French Exchange yourself, I'd try to go prepared), we can at least be sure of the fact that they will come our way eventually. All Christians experience periods when God seems far off, and instead of being a sign of failure, a divine hint that we've lost the plot, they are part of the essential rhythm of the Christian life.

Take Elijah, for example. The guy scored a tasty victory over the prophets of Baal by managing to slaughter a few hundred of them, but fled in fear when Jezebel threatened to have him killed: "Elijah was afraid and ran for his life. When he came to Beersheba in Judah, he left his servant there, while he himself went a day's journey into the desert. He came to a broom tree, sat down under it and prayed that he might die. 'I have had enough, Lord,' he said. 'Take my life; I am no better than my ancestors.' Then he lay down under the tree and fell asleep" (1 Kings 19:3-5).

Not exactly on a high, is he? Helpfully for us, his physical location even mirrors his spiritual one, and the best that he can hope for is a little shade from a desert shrub. But God knows the score and uses the sense of desperation to teach a valuable lesson. First, he provides for his physical needs, although this time in a different way than when the ravens brought him food. This is no-frills stuff as the bread and water just appear. The fuel gives him enough energy to carry on for the journey, and he makes his way to the mountain at Horeb where he expects to hear God. But the assumption throughout is that he was still in a desert, both physically and spiritually. Still, Elijah remained obedient and did what he was told, turning up at the mountain and waiting for God's voice. There's no sign in the tornado, no hint of it in the earthquake, and nothing the fire. Then comes the still, small voice.

> When Elijah heard it, he pulled his cloak over his face
> and went out and stood at the mouth of the cave. Then

a voice said to him, "What are you doing here, Elijah?"
He replied, "I have been very zealous for the Lord God
Almighty. The Israelites have rejected your covenant,
broken down your altars, and put your prophets to death
with the sword. I am the only one left, and now they are
trying to kill me too." The Lord said to him, "Go back
the way you came, and go to the Desert of Damascus.
When you get there, anoint Hazael king over Aram.
Also, anoint Jehu son of Nimshi king over Israel, and
anoint Elisha son of Shaphat from Abel Meholah to
succeed you as prophet. Jehu will put to death any who
escape the sword of Hazael, and Elisha will put to death
any who escape the sword of Jehu. Yet I reserve seven
thousand in Israel—all whose knees have not bowed
down to Baal and all whose mouths have not kissed
him." (1 Kings 19:13-18)

Why did God let him go through the desert? So that he could
hear God. And what did God say? "Go back the way you came,"
take a trip back through, make the experience come full circle,
and carry on God's work. Elijah's desert experience showed him
where to look for a successor as well as reminding him of his
place in life: not to feel great all the time, but to recognize God as
boss. Life may not always be a spiritual jackpot of tornadoes and
earthquakes, of giant moves of God, and of spectacular miracles.
Sometimes there is just silence, and it is then that we have to
listen out for God harder than ever.

David went through a similar experience which he describes in
Psalms 42 and 43. God is distant, and what's even worse is that
other people around have begun to notice the supposed divine
absence. Not only does David have to deal with the personal inse-

curity of feeling as though God has gone off air, he has to face up to the ridicule and cheek of others. What's more, he's one hundred miles away from Jerusalem, the home of the temple and the location of his most engaging encounters with God. Not a pleasant situation at all. But something changes, and what starts out as a "My tears have been my food day and night" dirge transforms itself into something else entirely, spreading over into Psalm 43:

> Vindicate me, O God, and plead my cause against an ungodly nation; rescue me from deceitful and wicked men. You are God my stronghold. Why have you rejected me? Why must I go about mourning, oppressed by the enemy? Send forth your light and your truth, let them guide me; let them bring me to your holy mountain, to the place where you dwell. Then will I go to the altar of God, to God, my joy and my delight. I will praise you with the harp, O God, my God. Why are you downcast, O my soul? Why so disturbed within me? Put your hope in God, for I will yet praise him, my Savior and my God. (Ps. 43:1-5)

We kick off with more of the same, the frustrations at being surrounded by "an ungodly nation" and feeling as though God has turned His back. But there's a solution. Instead of going backward, hiking it to Jerusalem to get high 'n' happy once more at some spirit-soaked temple worship, he opts to go forward. "Show me where to find you now," he says to God. "Lead me on." The point of this particular desert session is clear: to remind David to put his faith in God, not in the experience.

Desert experiences can offer all manner of good stuff to the willing Christian. Not only are they an opportunity to learn more about the character of both God and self, they remind us of the essential truth of following God: We are following God. Left to our own devices and good-vibe compasses, we'd never leave the temple. Doing it God's way is far more exciting, inspiring, and ultimately good for all. If we run away at the first sign of bad feelings, if we have failed to equip ourselves with a knowledge of God, and if we only value the big spiritual "event," then we run the risk of missing out on some absolutely vital parts of our relationship with God.

An Easy Life

There are other signs of Airhead influence besides this, and growing up with a distorted view of the Gospel is one of the biggest giveaways. Christianity is not supposed to be an easy ride. Yes, Jesus will give us rest; yes, He will give us strength. But rest and strength are not given so that we can spend as much time as we like by the pool. The aim of following Jesus is sadly not to get rich or comfortable, but to obey His commands. That means taking our cue from the master and picking up our own crosses. Again, this is not a hint for us all to start working on our very own messiah complexes. Instead, it is a reminder that we should not take the presence of pleasant feelings as a sign of spiritual success. If that were true, then Jesus' death would have been the ultimate failure. With that twisted logic in place we might as well pack up here then.

There Must Be More

There is a danger rooted in the fact that the Church's teenagers are now in uncharted waters. Many are second-generation charismatics, children of parents who have been into the scene for the majority of their children's lives and quite a bit of their own. We may wonder what the effects of using mobile telephones might be, and a similar wait is needed to answer questions about the Church's own young people. For those who have spent their lives "experiencing" God down in the front at meetings, is there a danger that they might develop Experience Fatigue? Might these people find themselves struggling to answer questions like "what next" and "what else" alone? For the generation above who have found in the charismatic experience a wonderful alternative to the stodgy spirituality of old, what will their children turn to in an effort to know God and be known by Him?

Playing a Game

The last thing that we want is for Christianity to be viewed as a game, but if what matters most is not lifestyle but a public show of emotion, then the pressure on others to exhibit the best signs leads us into trouble. It would be way too cynical—and way too wrong—to suggest that people believe Christianity is about raising your arms in the right way or exhibiting as much passion as possible during a worship session. But the desire to be accepted runs deep and strong in all of us. Of course, it's no big deal really, and our motives are always a bit of a mixed bag, but we must keep on pushing out the true story: that acceptance is not conditional on learning a set of moves. God's heart is far bigger than that.

No Responsibility

There may be a danger in living for the meetings and what goes on inside the Church that we try to let ourselves off the hook when it comes to our responsibilities as Christians. Working for justice, living an authentic life, and putting others first seem to lose their appeal in the face of fun, fun, fun at the latest conference. Living from one spiritual high to the next just misses the point of it all.

One Road, One Way

Perhaps one final consequence that points to a degree of influence might be a lack of accessibility that many people feel when coming into contact with Christians. Airheads are notoriously poor at accepting diversity, of accepting positions other than their own. For a few people the inability to fit in, whether it's by singing the songs, speaking the jargon, or adopting the attitudes, can leave them feeling just a little high and dry.

The Spirit of the Age

Surprising as it may be, there's more than a little that we Airhead Christians have in common with a certain element of popular culture. Take bimbos, for example. Like the made-up dolls spinning the Wheel of Fortune or giving us a twirl, things look great on the surface for the Airhead Christian. But scratch the surface, and what do you get? Marilyn Monroe puts it perfectly in *Some Like It Hot*; "not very bright I suppose," she says in her breathy, shoop-shoop-be-doop kind of voice. We get tempted to sign our names under the fickle and the vacuous instead of the meaningful and hard fought. We prefer the sugary treats of faith, especially when those treats are immediately accessible and cost us little in the way of effort. Like that other goddess among bimbos—Pamela Anderson—we can be tempted to put all our eggs in one basket. While they may not be quite as noticeable as Pammy's, the fact that we can feel God, that we can more often than not get a sense of Him can lead to the conclusion that the feelings are all that matters. Finally, in this current climate of changing cultural tides where everyone seems to be constructing their own hassle-free spirituality, does it seem just a little unfair that we've gotten stuck with all these rules and regulations? Why can't we have a break and ease off a little?

A Rally Cry for Misery?

Before we get too wound up about all this, it's worth taking a step back. This is certainly not an attempt at pushing the "God likes us miserable" line or a suggestion that the emotional should be distanced from the spiritual. Yes, there may be a few telltale signs of influence, perhaps even a little hint of decay, but there is no need to throw the baby out with the bath water. Much of the Airhead Christian point of view has roots in the most amazingly fantastic aspects of the evolution of the faith. What's more, it is precisely because Christianity is based on relationship rather than ritual that we even have the possibility for all this confusion in the first place. Feelings matter, experiences matter, knowing God matters, and all perform vital tasks in the relationship with God secured for us by Jesus. In a way the accusation that some Christians can be "too heavenly minded to do any earthly good" is a cause for celebration; the simple fact that we can enjoy a relationship with God, that works are not the building blocks of righteousness is a very good thing. Likewise the events around Pentecost show God fulfilling the promise made by Jesus (in John 14) that we would have "another counselor to be with [us] forever" (verse 16), living within us. Because of the presence of the Holy Spirit, the power and truth of God remain an active, accessible force available to all. That's not bad, is it?

Jesus, the Master Framer

If some of the reasons for the Airhead Christian are bound up with the mighty truth and goodness of God, what are we to do? Sit back and accept the drift away from dry land? Keep dosing up in the hope that we will magically stumble across the winning formula? No. The need is for balance, and for that we only have to look in one place.

Remember the quick look we took at Psalms 42 and 43? Well, N.T. Wright points out that there's a similar situation going on at the tail end of the Gospel of Matthew. The crucifixion is over, the body buried, but the disciples are confused as the tomb is suddenly empty. Actually "confused" is putting it just a little too mildly, as from the story about two of them walking to a village called Emmaus it would seem that "totally gutted" would be a more accurate description.

After the three most amazing days in human history, the doubts and questions had begun to take root. Perhaps it felt as if everything had gone wrong. The high of being around Jesus had vanished along with His body. Jesus Himself appeared to have been a fraud, and everyone in Jerusalem knew that the followers had been barking up the wrong tree all along. How depressing is that? It's the familiar post-experience low that the psalmist covered. But as the two of them are walking along the road absorbed in their own private grief, it doesn't look like they've got much chance of pulling themselves out of the hole. Until Jesus turns on the light:

> He said to them, "How foolish you are, and how slow
> of heart to believe all that the prophets have spoken!
> Did not the Christ have to suffer these things and then
> enter his glory?" And beginning with Moses and all the
> Prophets, he explained to them what was said in all the
> Scriptures concerning himself. As they approached the
> village to which they were going, Jesus acted as if he were
> going further. But they urged him strongly, "Stay with
> us, for it is nearly evening; the day is almost over." So he
> went in to stay with them. When he was at the table with
> them, he took bread, gave thanks, broke it and began to
> give it to them. Then their eyes were opened and they
> recognized him, and he disappeared from their sight.
> They asked each other, "Were not our hearts burn-
> ing within us while he talked with us on the road and

opened the Scriptures to us?" They got up and returned at once to Jerusalem. There they found the Eleven and those with them, assembled together and saying, "It is true! The Lord has risen and has appeared to Simon." Then the two told what had happened on the way, and how Jesus was recognized by them when he broke the bread. (Luke 24:25-35)

He'd listened patiently to the negative spin the two disciples had put on the story of His own death and life, but enough was enough. OK, so they'd managed to piece together the facts, the idea that Jesus was supposed to be the Messiah yet now He was dead, that people saying that His life was just a lot of fuss about nothing, but their conclusions about the story were way off center. Their reading was bound in with their feelings; everything felt wrong, nothing had worked. Jesus, on the other hand, told them a different story, piecing together the facts and breaking bread with them. He opened their eyes and showed them the way things really were. Back in Psalms 42 and 43, we read how the writer was longing for "light and truth" to help lead him out of his spiritual dry spell. This is just what the followers get: the truth about who Jesus was, the truth about what He did, and the chance to know Him, to feel Him, living inside their hearts by breaking bread and sharing communion with Him.

Isn't this sometimes the way it is with us? We get so caught up with our emotions that we confuse them with the truth. There was a terrible story some years ago about a handful of Christians who had been casting demons out of a man. The prayer session had lasted through the night and into the next day, only stopping when their attempts at getting rid of whatever they were trying to get rid of led them to jump up and down repeatedly on the man's chest. He died from the injuries.

If you'll forgive the jump in subject matter, I heard about a dog whose owner pretends to shoot the canine by pointing her finger at the dog and saying "bang." The dog immediately rolls over and plays dead. Nice trick. Of course, the dog doesn't know that it's the link between the owner's action and his that makes the whole trick so neat, and I wonder if he really did know that he was taking part in a simulated mock execution whether he'd be so keen. But that's beside the point; what matters is that there is no link in terms of meaning between what the woman does with her hand and the dog rolling over. It just so happens that the gun-shaped hand and "bang" are the triggers that the dog has learned; any command could have been chosen early on. The link between our feelings and what we perceive as the correct interpretation is just like Snuffle's Death Trick, something that we have learned to do. Why conclude that Jesus was a fraud just because we feel sad? Why give up on God just because we feel alone? Why jump on a man's chest just because we feel that's the way to get demons out? With the benefit of hindsight we can be almost guaranteed to see the full picture, but in the heat of the moment, well, that's a different story. That's where we need some other tools altogether.

What Tools Do We Need?

Corinth was one of those towns with a bit of a mad side to it. The constant presence of traders kept the mix of ideas and corruption nice and fresh, and the hundreds of prostitutes linked to the pagan temple did their own bit for local color. The town had such a reputation that the Greek verb "to Corinthianize" came to mean "to practice sexual immorality." And what of the church? Well, theirs was a tall order, and Paul's letters were aimed at specific areas that needed attention. It's not surprising that in such a town, things occasionally got a little fiery in the meetings, and Paul's words got straight to the heart of the matter:

> What then shall we say, brothers? When you come together, everyone has a hymn, or a word of instruction, a revelation, a tongue or an interpretation. All of these must be done for the strengthening of the church. If anyone speaks in a tongue, two—or at the most three—should speak, one at a time, and someone must interpret. If there is no interpreter, the speaker should keep quiet in the church and speak to himself and God. Two or three prophets should speak, and the others should weigh carefully what is said. And if a revelation comes to someone who is sitting down, the first speaker should stop. For you can all prophesy in turn so that everyone may be instructed and encouraged. The spirits of prophets are subject to the control of prophets. For God is not a God of disorder but of peace. (1 Cor. 14:26-33)

Is this Paul showing off his more anally retentive side? Has he taken out a subscription to *Control Freaks Monthly*? The simple fact is that Paul was giving them a framework within which to steer each meeting toward a sound goal: "the strengthening of the church." The fact that "everyone" seemed to be used to pitching in helps to paint the picture of a truly spontaneous and creative service, but with no structure in place there would have been a real threat of directionless wandering. According to Paul, there was a need for the church to learn to keep their wanderings on track and steward the emotions flying about the place. Perhaps the same advice could be taken up by ourselves? Should we only have the regulation number of prophecies, talks, and so on? Follow his advice to the letter? Not quite, as instead I wonder whether we ought to follow the spirit of the advice: that Christians need to retain a sense of focus about how we act. We're not in this for our own amusement; we're not here to feel better. Why not try working toward the strengthening of the Church, in all its glorious breadth?

But we can't stop here, can we? By just taking in support for this one side of the argument, we wander too near to the no man's land of selfishness. We have a remarkable ability to chuck tolerance out of the window when it comes to church, and for many the fact that a meeting might be filled with the sounds and sights of people expressing themselves in different ways can be enough to put them off for life. C.S. Lewis has Screwtape musing this one over in *The Screwtape Letters*. Writing as an experienced devil to his young nephew Wormwood, Screwtape's collection of letters allow C.S. Lewis to imagine just what Christianity might look like from "the other side":

> One of our great allies at present is the Church itself.
> Do not misunderstand me. I do not mean the Church
> as we see her spread out through all time and space and
> rooted in eternity, terrible as an army with banners.
> That, I confess, is a spectacle which makes out boldest
> tempters uneasy. But fortunately it is quite invisible to
> these humans. All your patient sees is the half-finished,
> sham Gothic erection on the new building estate. When
> he goes inside, he sees the local grocer with rather an
> oily expression on his face bustling up to offer him one
> shiny little book containing a liturgy which neither of
> them understands, and one shabby little book containing
> corrupt texts of a number of religious lyrics, mostly bad,
> and in very small print. When he gets into his pew and
> looks round him he sees just that selection of his neigh-
> bors whom he has hitherto avoided. You want to lean
> pretty heavily on those neighbors. Make his mind flit to

and fro between an expression like "the body of Christ" and the actual faces in the next pew.

We can be so uncomfortable with diversity, whether we're Airhead, Leadhead, or fresh off the guillotine. It makes for an uncomfortable ride, and while it's a little too late to get into demons and all that, the letter has a point: When we concentrate solely on our own annoyances, we completely fail see the Church as she is. Seated there, back row, arms crossed, and letting off bad vibes like a leaking nuclear reactor, we can't take church as anything other than a miserable experience. But this selfish position, this "but I don't like it" is just as narrow-minded and unadventurous as the free-wheeling feelings-junky. Remember the aim of the strengthening of the Church? Yes, we need to steward the emotions, but that includes the selfishly negative just as much as it does the mindlessly positive.

I wonder whether the salt that needs to accompany the pepper of keeping the emotions from directing the show might be this: going with the hunches. Here's Paul again: "Do not put out the Spirit's fire; do not treat prophecies with contempt. Test everything. Hold on to the good" (1 Thess. 5:19-21).

The line relates to the exercise of the gift of prophecy under the power and impulse of the Holy Spirit. Hearing God and letting others know about the whispers was rightly a big thing in the life of the early Church. It's probably got something to do with the fact that God just happens to be alive and is reasonably keen on doing something other than standing idly by while we scrabble around on earth trying to work out what to do next. Standing idly by is, in fact, a ridiculous accusation to lay at God's door; He who created, healed, judged, and saved a world, the one who is continually involved. We simply must be open to God's voice, open to His direction and molding. It's not even up for debate. Just as Jesus was gentle as a dove as well as being as wise as a serpent, we need to hold the tension between the hunch and the order, between the spontaneous and the thought-out.

How Should We Use Them?

But where does this leave us? It's all very well talking about church meetings and that, but how does this impact our own lives? I don't want to mention Toronto, but I can't avoid it. The year or two when things were going crazy over in a little church at the end of the Canadian city's main runway was a key landmark of recent years. With people taking trips to experience the Holy Spirit in a new and powerful way, returning to spread it about back at home, it didn't take long before many were talking of the amazing things that might come out of the whole experience. Excitement levels rose and expectation did likewise as thoughts eventually turned to the idea that perhaps even "revival" could be just around the corner.

So that's the outline, but what about the facts? This totally one-sided view is highly selective and probably shouldn't even be put on paper, but I wonder whether it might help as an illustration. You see, there was a church I knew. They were well into the Toronto thing; the leaders had all been there and returned full of passion and excitement. They immediately set up an open-ended series of Thursday night meetings, called Catch the Fire. It was so exciting, and the queues outside the door at 7:30 p.m. gave just a hint about the levels of expectation that packed the building out each week. And amazing things did happen. Bizarre things too. There were a few healings, some conversions, but mainly it felt as if the whole crowd were getting charged up. Charged up for what, no one could tell. But whatever was coming, it was bound to be big.

Meanwhile, life went on as usual. A local charity that worked with the homeless was getting ready for the coming winter by setting up a temporary night shelter for all the town's rough sleepers. As with every other year that this had happened, the local churches were invited to help out by providing volunteers for a particular night of the week. The job of the volunteers was to turn up from 8:00 p.m. to 10:00 p.m., help cook the meal, wash up, and chat with the residents. The church had always been supportive of the charity, and as before picked Thursday night as the one for which it would provide volunteers for the duration of the winter.

You can tell what happened. The Thursday night meetings were packed week in, week out while the church struggled to regularly get even two volunteers to turn up. Some were there, faithfully taking up what they saw as their responsibility, but sadly they were a minority.

If Toronto was a hunch, then going with it was a wise move. As for stewarding the emotions, well, in this isolated case viewed from the narrowest of perspectives, that just didn't really happen, did it? But forget Toronto, forget church meetings, forget structure, and all that. Think about the naked Christian, not the naked Church. What are God's blessings for? Why have the gifts been handed out? Is it all a matter of being able to check off an item on a list, to be able to say that we've "done" Toronto, that we've "done" Pensacola?

A guy who had "done" study of the law went to Jesus, trying to trick Him up with an awkward question. He's playing a game, but not just with Jesus. "Who is my neighbor?" he asks, drawing back the curtain on his heart. For him people are either in or out, either needing help or not deserving the time of day.

We all know the story: A man gets robbed and left for dead. Two shiny religious types—a priest and a Levite—walk on by, perhaps out of concern that if they touched the bleeding man they would make themselves ritually unclean. Perhaps they just couldn't be bothered. Anyway, the Jewish victim is lying by the road when a foreigner comes along, helps him to an inn, and picks up the tab while the victim recovers. A simple tale but a top-class one, too. "'Which of these three do you think was a neighbor to the man who fell into the hands of robbers?' The expert in the law replied, 'The one who had mercy on him.' Jesus told him, 'Go and do likewise'" (Luke 10:36-37).

The religious success story cannot even bring himself to say "the Samaritan," such is the strength of his racial hatred. But painting him as a bigoted racist lets ourselves off the hook. Who does God use? Yes, He uses us, but also the very ones we may consider unsuitable, unusable, and wholly unsavory.

Jesus was on His way to Jerusalem, getting ready for the final leg of His remarkable journey. Why tell the story at this particular point? A coincidence that He was heading the same way as the priest and the Levite? Was He trying to suggest that He was here to do things differently? You decide. But chew on this for a moment: stopping to help the victim was a hunch, just like the decision to pass by on the other side. "God wouldn't want it" may have been the logic going through the first two characters' minds. What was the hunch that prompted the Samaritan to help? "When he saw him, he took pity on him" (verse 33). Compassion, feeling, gut instinct—call it what you like—but God caught the Samaritan's attention through his emotions. But the story doesn't end there, not with an "oh, dear," an "I'm sorry," a few bandages, and a hasty exit. Instead the Samaritan "put the man on his own donkey, took him to an inn and took care of him. The next day he took out two silver coins and gave them to the innkeeper" (Luke 10:34-35). The gut feelings have become something else: further action. Not only has he spent time on the victim, being there for him the next day, but he has shelled out, too.

This is where our answer lies, this is how we implement Paul's advice to combine control with emotion. The hunch of stopping and the control of going with him show something that's almost profound: the two are not polar opposites, but intertwined, united, and sparking off each other. Out of the feelings comes the action, from the inspiration comes the response, with the God-given hunch there follows the self-molded response. Hearing and doing, receiving and going, feeling and acting, these are bound in and bonded together. They live, they thrive off each other. They are the hallmarks of the good neighbor, the clear sign that God's commands to love others as ourselves has been taken on board.

I'm glad of my Airhead past. I'm happy to have spent time learning to appreciate the feelings, but sad that for so much of that time I failed to see the next step. The feelings and experiences never got further than my own nerve endings. I failed to think beyond myself. I failed to see the wider picture. Feelings are not here for our benefit alone, and the same can be said of knowledge, experience, and even action. The aim is not our own satisfaction, but the strengthening of the Church. But wait a minute. That word *church*—instead of the faces in your Sunday local, turn your mind to something else: "Spread out through all time and space and rooted in eternity, terrible as an army with banners." I'll say it for the last time: This is God's battle, not ours. It's time we put our armor on. It's time we got naked.

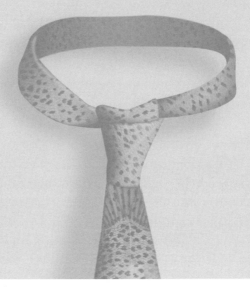

Appendix A

Naked Christian
A Six-Week Bible Study Guide

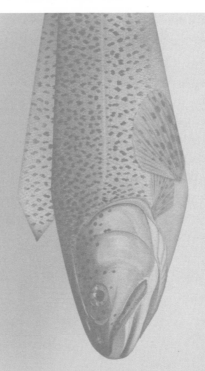

1

Legally Holy

Why Being 'Nicely Spiritual' Isn't Enough

MATTHEW 5:17-20

In 57 Words ...

If only Christianity were all about the presentation. If churches commended their congregation like judges at a synchronized swimming competition, then we'd all have an easier time of it, yes? A few toothy smiles could go a long way, but a passage like this underlines just how far short our interpretations of Jesus' message can leave us.

It's Like ...

I was helping out in a Sunday school meeting once, and my ears pricked up just before the worship started. The leader—a nice guy, I'd like to say—was telling the assorted eleven- and twelve-year-olds about how they'd get a sweet if they "worshipped properly." I was a little confused, but pleased when one sparky young thing asked *how*, exactly, they could tell whether the crew was toeing the line worship-wise. "Oh," said the leader. "Don't worry; we can tell. Like if you've got your eyes shut or are *really* singing." The leader looked pleased with himself. The boy looked unimpressed.

It's crazy what we do to Christianity. We turn a living, breathing relationship into a set of rules and techniques. Yeah, I understand why the leader said what he did, but he'd missed the point, and everyone else in the room knew it—especially the kids.

What the Bible Says ...

The Sermon on the Mount (a sound teaching session from The Master, from which this passage is taken) deals with just this problem. The "spiritual" success stories (the Pharisees) had become so nicely religious that Jesus simply had to step in. Here He is not slating the laws themselves, but addressing the problem of people making a big deal of sticking to them in public, yet breaking them with their hidden attitudes. The next four study sessions from Matthew 5 deal with this.

But My Closet's So Full of Stuff ...

We have a problem. We all suffer—humanity always has and probably always will. It's called ego, and it's part of our very makeup. Leaf through the Old Testament, and you will see how many of the stories deal with the situation of men and women thinking more of themselves than is appropriate. We love to inflate our image, to give ourselves top billing, to believe that the world revolves around us. This, you see, is a problem. Jesus tackled it with these Pharisees, people who had become so convinced that what mattered was being good at doing religious things, forgetting that their hearts were also part of the deal. We can be just the same, whether it's rating ourselves as "performers" or players on the Christian scene or getting wound up because things just aren't going our way. We'd save ourselves a lot of hassle if we tried a little harder to prevent things from getting out of perspective.

So It's Time to Think ...

What areas are you wound up by at the moment? Stop. Think. Pray. Make a list of your grievances, the things you resent God for. It may seem trivial, or it may seem like too much to handle all at once. Either way, ask God to show you where you might have gotten hold of the wrong version of the story. Then think: Are you really so wronged by God?

And Time to Talk ...

When it comes down to it, we all allow our egos to get in the way from time to time. What lessons do you know from the Bible where other people go though the same thing? What do you learn from them?

And Pray ...

Sometimes it's good to be alone, contemplating the natural world around you. Let your mind focus on the miraculous way in which God's creation gets on perfectly well without man's grubby little mitts smeared all over it.

And Get Naked ...

The finest of all God's miracles is this: that we, who count so little in the big scheme of things, are worth paying so dear a price for.

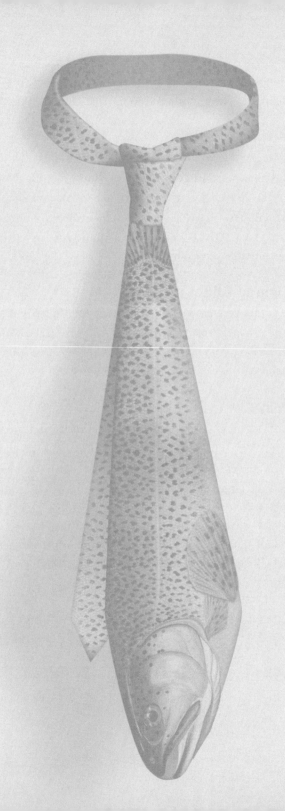

2

Week Two:

Jesus and the Uncomfortable Truth
Why Honesty Hurts and Helps

MATTHEW 5:21-26

In 41 Words ...

Jesus never came to earth to pat us on the back and turn a blind eye to our faults: this was no mere morale-boosting PR trip by the Almighty. Instead, Jesus came to present the truth, however uncomfortable that might be.

It's Like ...

Well, of course, we can all feel pretty smug and comfortable about a line like, "Do not murder." As far as the commandments go, it's one of the easiest to stick to (certainly much safer than all that tricky stuff about oxen and wives). But Jesus' audiences—both then and now—share a tendency to miss the point. Once again Jesus goes right to the heart of the matter, relating the issue of murder to its all-important root: anger. It's too easy to let ourselves off the hook, to see the Gospel painted in big brush strokes rather than focusing in on the fine detail. It simply is not enough to "be a good person," to go through life without cheating on a tax return. We have to face up to the fact that Jesus calls us to look long and hard at the roots of sin.

What the Bible Says ...

This whole "you have heard it said" line ... well, it could be a little confusing. Some trip up on it, believing that it's a case of Jesus contradicting what was said in the Old Testament. In fact it refers to the interpretation put on the old Scriptures by those with religious power. Yet again, Jesus is not afraid of bringing people back into line, regardless of power or importance.

But My Closet's So Full of Stuff ...

Can we take this passage as one that slates all those who are happy to reject Christianity in favor of being a "good person"? Can we take it as further ammunition against those who wear robes and beards? No. This comes right back at us, a measuring stick against which we must place our own lives and attitudes. Jesus doesn't outlaw us getting angry, having conflicts, or speaking strongly. Instead, in all these things, we have simply got to watch out for hatred and animosity. It's not an easy, natural, or even a particularly human way to act. But you know what? It sure is a godly way of going about things.

So It's Time to Think ...

Perhaps it might be time to hand out a few heartfelt apologies. Who have you wounded—either deliberately or unintentionally?

And Time to Talk ...

When does anger become sin? When is it OK?

And Pray ...

Jesus gets to the root of murder—uncontrolled and vindictive anger. How's your temper? How's your language?

And Get Naked ...

Are you good at making peace? What three steps could you take to improve your success rate? How could you make the next twenty-four hours different?

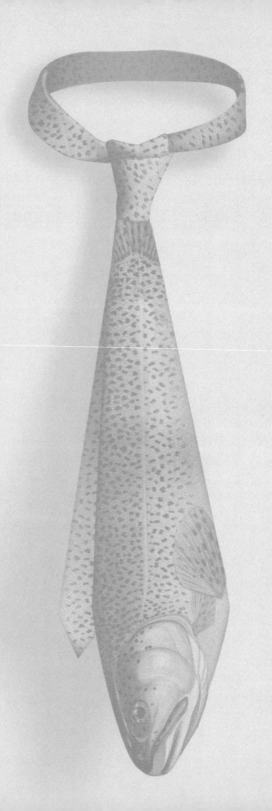

3

It's All in the Mind
Why Sin Has Teeth

MATTHEW 5:27-30

In 67 Words ...

It's the most powerful muscle, the most potent sexual organ, and the most complex device we possess. Contrary to the opinion of various foot-chewing weirdoes—and you know by now that I'm writing as a recovering foot-chewing weirdo—the brain *is* a vital ingredient in our relationship with God. It's not all about feelings, and we can't discount the role our minds play in our Christian living.

It's Like ...

Take even the briefest of glimpses at the news, and you'll see multiple examples of people trying to shrug off the responsibility for their actions, staring bewilderedly at the chaos of their lives that surrounds them, scratching their heads, and wondering, "How on earth did things get like *this*?" Whether it's the person caught cheating on their partner or the company boss convicted of cooking the books, we've got a remarkable natural talent for shifting the blame away from ourselves whenever we feel the heat coming from around the corner. The simple truth is that what might start as seemingly innocent thoughts—the dabble in the pool of lust while awaiting a number 56 bus, the rehearsal of devastating put-downs after we've been embarrassed—can so easily become the roots of something far worse. "It's all in the mind" is one of those phrases we throw around so lightly, without pausing to recognize just how massively true it actually is.

What the Bible Says ...

In this passage we see Jesus once again getting stuck into the heart of the matter. Here's the deal: Sexual immorality isn't just about what goes on physically; it's about what goes on mentally. By making it crystal clear that we should not look at each other as sex objects, Jesus is underlining the humanity of everybody. Women are not here for men's pleasure, not here to titillate, to serve, or to be toyed with. As followers of Jesus, our eyes, mind, and hearts have to be pure.

But My Closet's So Full of Stuff ...

Of course, this is not easy—Jesus knew that. But that's why He calls for drastic action, which we see in verses 29 and 30. This imagery is not to be taken literally, but the message is clear: Don't play with fire, and don't put yourself in places where you are going to be tempted.

So It's Time to Think ...

Look around you: Are you undermining the humanity of others? Do we see people as objects rather than people? We need to deal with this.

And to Talk ...

Is it OK to have different standards than others with regard to this? Are there some boundaries that we all ought to share?

And Pray ...

This is not a game we're talking about. Whatever you've been involved in up to this point, make up your mind right now to make a choice for purity, both when you're around others and when you're at home.

And Get Naked ...

Just in case you're wondering, God loves the sinner who turns back to Him. Remember the prodigal son?

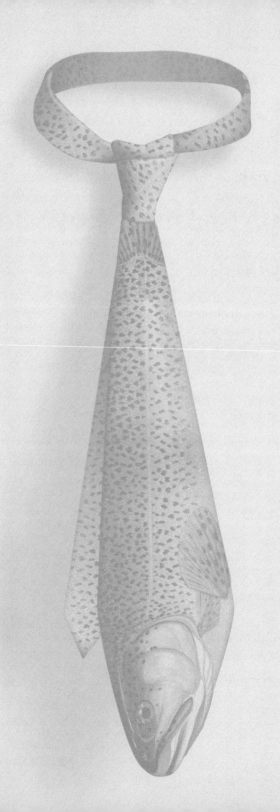

4

God of the People
Why God Quite Likes Us

MATTHEW 5:31-32

In 34 Words ...

How does God feel about you? Perhaps you might find it a little hard to say, but spend a little while thinking and looking in the Psalms for evidence of His attitude toward you.

It's Like ...

We've all been made to feel small at some time. For me it was Joanne Clarke, and I was ten. I fancied her. She invited me to her party. I was happy. She invited me so that her friend would have someone to talk to while she made out with older boys. I didn't fancy Joanne's friend. I didn't have a good time. The way we treat people matters, whether it's the breakdown of a lifelong relationship or a passing encounter with a stranger. Relationships are high on God's agenda.

What the Bible Says ...

The passage starts with the quote about how divorce was previously sealed by the giving of a written paper. This law was introduced back in the days of Moses (see Deut. 24:1-4) and was a way of guarding against a reckless and disposable attitude held by some men to their marriages. But as we see, Jesus came to add to the previous laws, to model a way in which a relationship with God was to go deeper, to impact the life on a massively fundamental level. This whole passage bangs out a clear message: Life with Jesus is not about just following laws in some legalistic way. Instead it's about applying the full breadth of the spirit of those laws to every aspect of our lives.

But My Closet's So Full of Stuff ...

The deal is this: Life with Christ is not about being a slave to the law. The fact is that we cannot walk away from relationships, we cannot treat them as a transaction or contract. This is the great truth behind Jesus' message—that relationships matter and people are worth sacrifice. Jesus' message was delivered to God's people in person precisely because it communicated a change in tactic, a new way for God's people to relate to their Creator. It's a personal thing, and the sooner we realize it, the better things get in our lives. Forget being able to do all manner of spiritual gymnastics—what's important is how your life with Jesus and others is lived, not how often you've been on a Christian platform, how loud you can speak in tongues or how many Bible verses you can quote.

So It's Time to Think ...

Leaving aside the idea of divorce, can you think of any occasions where you've treated relationships as disposable, where people have been treated with a dignity less than that which they truly deserved? Might it be time to make those right?

And to Talk ...

What other occasions are there in the Bible where Jesus develops a law from the Old Testament? What do they tell us about the heart of God?

And Pray ...

What has been the result of God's offer of a relationship to you? How has it changed your life? Tell Him loud and clear. Write it, sing it, paint it, whisper it.

And Get Naked ...

Is there any room in your life for taking that relationship with God just a little deeper?

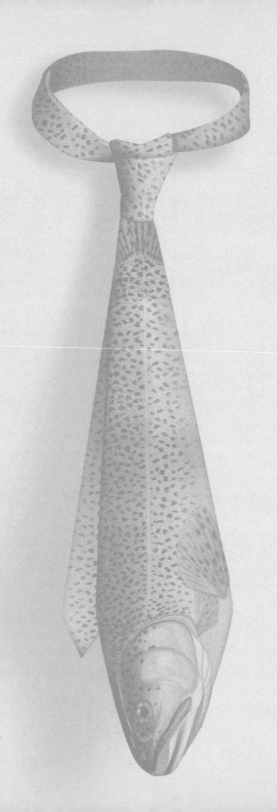

5

Honesty

Why It's Not a Good Idea to Talk About People, Even Though It Seems Like Fun at the Time

MATTHEW 5:33-37

In 75 Words ...

The Bee Gees. What a fine group. They gave so much, including the lines: "It's only words, and words are all I have, lah lah lah lah lah lah." I'll tell you what: They may have given us some quality tunes, but in this instance they're fully wrong. In life it's never a case of it being only words. Words are important. Very important. Which is where a lot of problems seem to come in.

It's Like ...

From the playground to the courtroom, the tongue is the daddy of all weapons. Remember that line, "Sticks and stones may break my bones, but words will never hurt me?" What a load of crap. If ever there was a potential for lasting damage, it can be found in the lashings we hand out with our tongues.

"But," you say, "I'm OK as I don't talk about people behind their backs. Much." Personally I've actually given up saying this, but not because I've cleaned up my act. The truth is that I still struggle. I gossip. I'm opinionated and arrogant. I'm rude about people. It's not all the time, and I try to kid myself that, when it happens, it's just me being funny, ironic, or honest. But I'm wrong. Sin is sin, and I'm guilty.

This is where the problems start: It's all too easy for us to dial down the guilt when it comes to the stuff that our tongues offer up to the waiting world. And just like in the rest of the Sermon on the Mount, Jesus is keen to offer a lesson that steers us away from feeling like we're off the hook if we don't have a mouth like a sailor or haven't been sued for slander in the last six months. Yet again we see that Jesus' standards are a tad higher. We cannot gloss over "the little sins" if we hope to have any type of integrity in our lives.

What the Bible Says ...

This passage has plenty of insight into the culture of the day, but that whole thing about swearing oaths might be a tad removed from life in the twenty-first century. But there's a part that we can all nod along to: It can be hard to let our "yes" be yes and our "no" be no. Many of us find it hard to say "no" to things, often because we don't want to let people down. Of course, this can easily get us in more trouble than we had hoped, all because we lack the guts or security in the first place.

But My Closet's So Full of Stuff ...

The truth is that God is a God of truth. In Him there is no hint of a lie. And, you guessed it, we should be aiming in the same direction.

So It's Time to Think ...

The great thing about a relationship with Jesus is that there's always encouragement to keep on working on our character. Some get a little despondent at the sight of their failings, anxious that they will never reach our Savior's standards. That is to miss the point: It's more about the direction we're traveling rather than the destination we reach. So try a personal audit; look out for the lies (yes, even the "white" ones), root out the over-commitments, and highlight the slander.

And to Talk ...

When facing up to the truth about ourselves, how easy is it to be vulnerable and honest with others? What helps to support us when we're trying to do this?

And Pray ...

When people hear our words and watch our lives, do they see a reflection of the true God?

And Get Naked ...

Why don't you fill this bit in: What's God's message to you on all this?

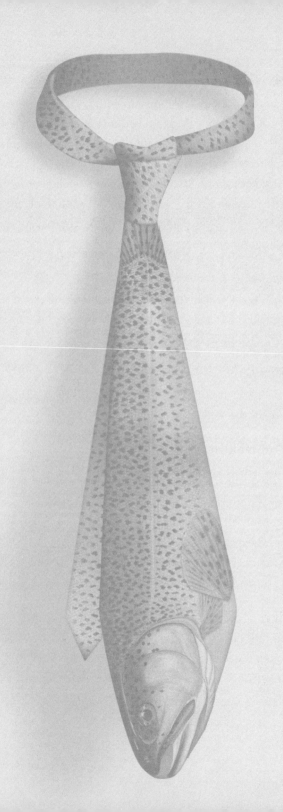

6

Week Six:

The Final Word

Why We Must Put Faith into Action

EXODUS 3:7-10

In 97 Words ...

This little study guide has brought up some chunky issues of personal integrity, but there's a bigger picture that we simply cannot avoid. Jesus commanded us to "go," to love Him, to serve the poor, and to spread His crazily upside-down message. Yet we don't have to wait until we're all sorted before we can take up the challenge. Like we said, God uses us as well as our failings. So as we run out of ink, it's time to be honest. After all, what's the point of getting naked if we're not going to go outside?

It's Like ...

Consider this fact: Today there are 2.8 billion people who have to get through the next twenty-four hours with less than two dollars. A third of them will face the challenge with just one dollar to their name. As a result thirty-thousand children will die by this time tomorrow. So let's start by considering a question: Do you ever feel helpless, as if the enormity of global injustice easily outmatches your ability to change it? Spend time on this one, working out what that helplessness feels like. How do you normally respond to these feelings?

What the Bible Says ...

1. What was life like for the Israelites?

2. Can you join the dots between the Israelites' oppression and the realities of life for the 2.8 billion poor people in the world?

3. How should we respond to this situation?

4. To what extent do you think that because we have a democratic right to speak up on these issues it is therefore our obligation to do so?

5. Moses had some decent political leverage. How can we make our views known?

6. What type of response from God do you think Moses might have been expecting?

7. In what ways are you wholly unqualified for the task ahead?

But My Closet's So Full of Stuff ...

Can we ever do enough? Of course not. Should we strive for improvement? Absolutely. But in acknowledging our weakness, can we also praise God? Can we thank Him for our utter dependence on His mercy? Can we get just a little bit excited about the fact that we have the opportunity to be involved in things that bear the fingerprints of the Almighty Creator?

So It's Time to Think ...

What did God need from Moses: ability or obedience? Where do your tastes lie? What's your flavor—would you rather be talented than serve humbly? Write a list of all your attributes in these two areas: the gifts God has given you and the times when you have obeyed His commands and followed His plan. How's the balance?

And to Talk ...

Read Matthew 25:31-46 and think about it carefully.

1. When did you last see Jesus hungry, thirsty, a stranger, naked, sick, or in prison?

2. What was your reaction?

3. Have a look at the way your life is structured, in terms of days, weeks, and months. Does it give you opportunities to see Jesus or does it keep Him at a distance?

And Pray ...

Grace, mercy, and the challenge to follow Christ. How great a deal is that?

And Get Naked ...

How can you be the "you" at the heart of God's plan?

Craig Borlase was born in 1972 and grew up in Chorleywood, England. He left his faith behind to go to university, where he studied English Literature, returning to it a little later inspired by God, friendships, and the revolution that had taken place within his old youth group, Soul Survivor. He edited their magazine, helped write their books, and played their songs. He has taught in schools, written books on lifestyle, the Bible, social justice, and music, and is trying to pursue a faith that counts. He lives outside London with his wife and daughter.

www.craigborlase.com

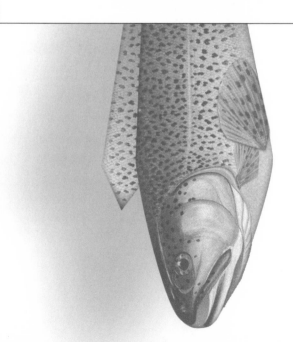

[RELEVANT**BOOKS**]

FOR MORE INFORMATION ABOUT OTHER RELEVANT BOOKS,
check out *www.relevantbooks.com.*